HINTERLAND

Hinterland offers an answ[er]
question 'what is creative
by showcasing the best ne[w]
the fields of memoir, essay, travel and
food writing, reportage, psychoscape,
biography, flash non-fiction and more.

Our pages bring together work by
established, award-winning authors
alongside new writers, many of whom
we are thrilled to publish for the first time
and whose work, we promise, will merit
your full attention.

Often, the pieces you'll find in Hinterland
will straddle the boundaries between
strands and be difficult to classify:
we see this as a strength. Hinterland
intends to challenge, move, entertain
and, above all, be a fantastic read.

WELCOME TO ISSUE 10

Advocates for Hinterland:
Nathan Hamilton, Kathryn Hughes,
Helen Smith, Rebecca Stott, Ian Thomson

Editorial Team
Editors-In-Chief – Yin F. Lim & Andrew Kenrick
Art Direction & Design – Tom Hutchings
Business Support – Ben Watkins
Proofreaders – Susan K. Burton, Aaron Deary, Margaret Hedderman,
              Stephen Massil, Florence Pearce-Higginson,
              Claire Reiderman, Yianni Theochari and Isabel Williams
Founding Editors – Freya Dean & Andrew Kenrick

Submissions
Hinterland is committed to paying writers and artists for all work we publish.
Please send us your work via Submittable:
hinterlandnonfiction.submittable.com
We accept submissions year-round and endeavour to reply within 4 months.
We regret we are unable to provide feedback.
There is a small fee of £3 per submission.

Subscriptions
An annual subscription to Hinterland (four issues, print and digital)
costs £40 U.K., £44 Europe, £54 Rest-of-world.
Digital subscription only, £20.
Please visit our website for full details.

Distribution
Hinterland is distributed worldwide by NBN International.
For all trade orders contact +44 (0) 1752 202301
orders@nbninternational.com

Advertising
Please see our website for current rates, or to discuss sponsorship please
contact us at hinterlandnonfiction@gmail.com

Acknowledgments
The Editors gratefully acknowledge financial contributions from
the UEA Publishing Project.

Find Hinterland online at
www.hinterlandnonfiction.com
or contact us: hinterlandnonfiction@gmail.com

ISBN: 978-1-913861-67-4
ISSN (Print): 2632-136X
ISSN (Online): 2632-1378

HINTERLAND

THE BEST NEW CREATIVE NON-FICTION

Issue 10
2022

Issue 10

FLASH NON-FICTION

COVER

Contributors

Tom Bailey *(Throwing the Dice Again)* grew up in London and studied Creative Writing at Boston University. He was awarded a Robert Pinsky Global Fellowship in 2020, and is currently trying to put together his first pamphlet. His poems have been published in *bath magg, The Kindling, Hawk & Whippoorwill, The Cormorant,* and the Munster Literature Centre's *Poems from Pandemia Anthology.*

Susmita Bhattacharya *(In the Spotlight)* is an Indian-born writer. Her debut novel, *The Normal State of Mind* (Parthian, 2015) was longlisted at the Mumbai Film Festival, 2018. Her short story collection, *Table Manners* (Dahlia Publishing, 2018), won the Saboteur Award for Best Short Story Collection, was a finalist for the Hall & Woodhouse DLF Prize and has been featured on BBC Radio 4. Susmita teaches creative writing at Winchester University and facilitates the ArtfulScribe Mayflower Young Writers programme in Southampton. She was also Writer-in-Residence at London's Word Factory in 2021. Find her on Twitter @Susmitatweets

Constance Kresge
(Maintaining An Ambivalent Art: Caring) works as a freelance business consultant and virtual Chief of Staff. She has been taking writing classes off and on for years and is thrilled to be published for the first time in *Hinterland*. She lives in Washington, D.C. with her husband, toddler and demanding but lovable rescue dog. When not creating to-do lists, spreadsheets or trying to write, she loves to hike – preferably in the Rocky Mountains.

Tom Hutchings is our in-house graphic designer, responsible for the layout and title pages in this very journal. Every issue he has to write this bio and every issue it is almost impossible. Worse, he has to wonder if anyone ever reads it. Why would they, he thinks. Anyway, if you have read this far, why not look at his other work on thorngraphicdesign.com

Bonnie Lander Johnson *(Treasure)* is Fellow and Director of Studies in English at Newnham College, Cambridge. Her academic books on early modern literature are *Chastity in Early Stuart Literature and Culture, Blood Matters, Shakespeare's Plants* and *The Cambridge Handbook to Literature and Plants.* She is now working on a biography of Shakespeare, a memoir and a fenland farming novel. In 2022 her short story 'Idolatry' was short-listed for the V.S. Pritchett Prize.

Christopher Linforth *(The Estranged)* is the author of three story collections: *The Distortions* (Orison Books, 2021), winner of the 2020 Orison Books Fiction Prize, *Directory* (Otis Books/ Seismicity Editions, 2020) and *When You Find Us We Will Be Gone* (Lamar University Press, 2014).

Rob McClure Smith's *(Wee Kenny: Poet Maudit)* work has appeared in *Gettysburg Review, New Ohio Review, StoryQuarterly, Manchester Review, Chicago Quarterly, Barcelona Review* and other literary magazines. His novel, *Cowan*, won the Black Springs Crime Fiction Prize and is forthcoming later this year. He teaches film at Knox College in Galesburg, Illinois where he is John and Elaine Fellowes Distinguished Chair in English.

Reece Reilly *(Stoic Indifference)* is an artist and printmaker based on the east coast of Norfolk. With a strong focus on collage and colour and a love of awkward composition; his work explores ideas of perception and interaction. Instagram: @reece_reilly

Zachary D. Shell *(To: remain.)* lives in Denver, Colorado, where he teaches seventh grade Language Arts and dreams of going back to Ecuador. If he's not singing with his barbershop chorus, you can find him writing at his favourite local coffee shop. Now. You can find him there right now.

Charlie J. Stephens *(When They Took All The Trees)* is a non-binary, mixed race fiction writer living on unceded Chochenyo Ohlone land in Northern California. Charlie has lived all over the US as a bike messenger, wilderness guide, book seller and seasonal shark diver (for educational purposes only). Charlie's work has appeared in *Electric Literature, Peculiar, The Racket, Fresh.Ink* and *Original Plumbing* among others. Charlie has recently finished a collection of short stories, and is hard at work on their first novel. More at charliejstephenswriting.com and on Instagram @charliejstephenswriting.

Born in New York, **Stephanie Tam** *(Speaking in Tongues)* is a writer, researcher and audio producer. She has worked for various radio shows and media companies, including Freakonomics, Radiolab and First Look Media. Her writing has been featured in a number of outlets including *The Believer, Behavioral Scientist* and *Slate*. Before journalism, she explored her love for storytelling and the social sciences through two masters in world literatures and social policy respectively at the University of Oxford as a Daniel M. Sachs Scholar. She also graduated with distinction from the MFA in Creative Writing at the University of East Anglia.

Anna Vaught *(What I saw will not be what I see)* is a novelist, essayist, short fiction writer, editor, secondary English teacher, mentor, campaigner and author of four books, including 2020's *Saving Lucia* and *Famished*. Her work is published in journals, anthologies and national press and she has been a monthly columnist for *The Bookseller*. Her new novel, *The Zebra and Lord Jones*, is on agency submission, while a book on writing, *The Alchemy*, is launching with Unbound. Anna's second story collection, *Ravished*, is published by Reflex Press this year as well as her memoir, *These Envoys of Beauty*, in 2023. Anna speaks as a guest university lecturer and is a tutor for Jericho Writers.

Jack Young *(The Boy Next Door)* writes experimental fiction and non-fiction, which has found its home with *Entropy, Somesuch Stories, 3 A:M, Caught by the River* and *Burning House Press*, among others. He also co-hosts the literary podcast *Tender Buttons* with Storysmith Books. His hybrid chapbook of interspecies intimacies *Urth* was published in 2022 by Big White Shed. He is currently curating a participatory programme at Bristol's *Spike Island Gallery* around the concept of the Body-Forest, which is a way of decentering the human and thinking ecologically about desire, time, language, community and more.

Guidelines for submissions

- Submissions should be made via Submittable only. Please follow the link below..

- A small fee of £3 per submission applies to non-subscribers. Subscribers enjoy the benefit of submitting their work for free.

- All work should be new, previously unpublished material. If your work is subsequently accepted elsewhere, please kindly let us know.

- Pieces should not run to more than 5000 words. We accept anything from 500 words (very short pieces will be considered for our flash non-fiction slot). We also accept extracts from longer works, or works in progress.

- We warmly embrace writing on any topic, or from any genre, we ask only that it falls somewhere in the realm of non-fiction writing.

- Your work will be considered for all upcoming issues; it might help you to know that we operate a 3-4 month editorial lead time.

- We regret that, due to the number of submissions received, we cannot provide feedback.

hinterland.submittable.com/submit

Editorial

Essays have traditionally been associated with argument and persuasion, but the ones we receive as a creative non-fiction magazine do not fit neatly into this description. If anything, they are exploratory by nature, and defy definition and categorisation.

While we continue to grapple with the concept, Issue 10 celebrates the essay that is 'an open-ended adventure, an invitation to doubt and self-surprise', as described by essayist Phillip Lopate.

The essays in this issue also use the form as a platform for a multitude of voices to ring clear: Anna Vaught's exploration of how nature and determination helped her survive complex and extended trauma. S.Y. Tam's reflection on language and identity as she invites us to join an Esperanto convention. Bonnie Lander Johnson drawing on her archival research into the past to make sense of her

Yin F Lim spent many years as a journalist writing other people's stories before deciding to write her own. She completed a Creative Non-Fiction MA at the University of East Anglia and now mainly writes about family, food and migration.

present. Constance Kresge pondering on parenting, work and the limitations life places on us and our creativity. Tom Bailey considering the last lines of poems. Zachary Shell remembering a turning point in his own life, and that of musician Otis Redding.

As well as personal essays, Issue 10 also features a selection of powerful flash nonfiction from Susmita Bhattacharya, Christopher Linforth and Charlie J. Stephens around pivotal moments with relationships, and stories by Rob McClure Smith and Jack Young that centre on the trials of youth.

As you dive into the essays and stories in this issue, we hope you will discover how their 'unexpected turns would lift the prose and make it sing', as Lopate says, and agree with us that they're among the best new creative non-fiction writing we've come across.

The Editors

Andrew Kenrick has worked as an archaeologist and an archivist, a writer and an editor. He is currently studying for a PhD at the University of East Anglia, where he also teaches English Literature and Publishing.

The Estranged

by Christopher Linforth

I study absent fathers. Missing. Wayward. Drunk.
I read memoirs and academic articles about them
and wonder about my own. He left England fifteen
years ago for France. I heard he wanted to start a
new life after his stint in prison.

—

For the first time in years, I google my father's name
to see what has become of him. Straight away I find
a strange website – everything is in French – that lists
hundreds of names and the words *Décès en France*. It
takes a moment for me to realize that the page has a
record of my father's death in the summer. I double-
check the birthdate and the spelling of his middle name.
They match. Even so, I can barely believe it is him.

—

Years ago, I wrote an anonymous letter to the police
about my father downloading child pornography. At the
time, it seemed the easiest way to handle the situation.
I did not live with him; he lived with a relative and
her young daughter. I could not stand to see where
this housing arrangement would end up. I mailed the
letter on the way to the airport for a summer job in the
US. I had no desire to be around for the aftermath.

———

At home, in Oklahoma, I drift around my house in shock. My numb state surprises me — I had always presumed I would feel relief. But I don't. Late at night, I call the hospital in central France. No one speaks English. I try several days in a row until someone takes pity on my situation and puts me through to a woman who can understand what I am asking. She provides me with some information and a promise that a doctor in oncology will email me. Her mention of oncology unnerves me. Almost every member of my family has died from a stroke or some related complication. Cancer has never been a cause of death before.

———

Halfway through my summer job placement in North Carolina, I got an email from a cousin telling me I must call home. I ignored it. A second message said it was an emergency. I did nothing. Follow-up emails begged me. Finally one said: *Your father has been arrested.* I still waited a couple of days before I called. I explained that I had been unable to access my inbox. Password troubles. There was doubt in the woman's voice. She demanded that I come back to England. I demurred, then told her that I would think about it.

———

I contact a notaire to deal with my father's estate. I wait for days for a reply. I stress over how I am going to deal with his house, his bills, his pension. Where do I even start? Then I think about the location of his body: is it at the hospital morgue or someplace else? Would it have decomposed by now? I find a friend on social media who is fluent in French. She makes some inquiries on my behalf. Finally, I hear from a counselor at the hospital. She tells me of my father's death; his fall in his house, his metastatic cancer, his refusal of treatment. She explains that his body was cremated and the remains shipped back to a relative in England. She puts me in contact with the English solicitor handling his estate.

—

After my father's arrest, I never saw him again. My relatives did and they forgave him in time. I could not. He was a drunk and a bully and, I suspected, a recidivist. I returned to the US for graduate school and then a job. I turned my back on England and the relatives still friendly with my father. I was happy with my new life: my girlfriend and my writing career, such as it was. I had no reason to return to my homeland.

—

My father left me nothing in his will. Though he lived in France, he disinherited me under English law. He left a letter with the solicitor that outlined his case for excluding me: I was estranged. Not him, but me. This was his attempt at revenge; he must have worked out I had sent the letter to the police. After all, I had refused to cut short my time in North Carolina all those years ago and few other people could have known what my father was downloading.

—

I own a single picture of my father. He wears a shirt and tie, a briefcase raised to shield his face. But you can see the discomfort in his eyes, his shock of unruly gray hair. A local news photographer took the shot as my father walked to the courthouse. The picture sits in the depths of my computer files. Hidden. Rarely looked at. Ready to be found by someone else. ◧

In the Spotlight

by Susmita Bhattacharya

I started piano lessons when I was eight years old.
I hated those lessons. My teacher, a middle-aged
Parsi gentleman, would breathe hotly down my
neck, a long pencil in hand, ready to smack my
knuckles if I stumbled over the keys. He'd rage
in my ears and scratch my book with angry lines
where I just couldn't play the notes accurately. The
whole week would be a build-up to that one hour on
Saturday mornings when I would have to face him.
At home, when I practised, I was fine. On Monday,
my scales would be perfect. Arpeggios melodious.
Pieces balanced and accurate. Then, on Friday,
it would all go downhill; the scales a shamble of
sounds and my piece unrecognisable.

He taught us on a beautiful grand piano: black
and sleek, brass strings glinting in the morning
sunshine that slanted into the living room. There
was also a digital piano, one of the first of its
kind, in that tiny room. The walls were covered
in atmospheric oil paintings; I'd stare at them to
escape from the yelling and threats until I knew
every brush stroke, every colour on the canvas.

Finally, after four years of torture and a complete
hatred for music, I quit. I revolted against my piano
lessons and swore never to return to them. But I
realised I missed it. I'd play the piano at home but
wanted to learn more. My parents looked around

for another tutor. A gentler person. Someone who could reinstil the love and confidence I had lost over the years.

Soon, I was attending piano lessons again. There were no foot-long pencils to rap my knuckles with my new teacher, who was kind and patient with me. Slowly, she built up my confidence to play again and to believe in myself as a pianist. My books were no longer vandalised with red pencil and shame. Slowly, I learnt to love and play music again.

I began to perform in local concerts. The music ensemble evenings, every three months, were something I'd look forward to. I'd play my little pieces – Harebell, Spring Song, Ode to Joy – and I began pushing myself to learn tougher pieces. Beethoven. Chopin. Mozart. The thrill of being able to play a Grade 6 piece when I was still doing Grade 4 exams gave me a real high. Then I managed to get a place to perform at the annual music concert, on the big stage. I had decided on Mozart's Fantasia in D Minor, my most difficult piece yet. I waited in the green room, fingers stretched and nervous. Heart beating erratically. I had to pull it off without any mistakes. I shut my eyes, trying to get myself in the mood. I was going up soon.

When I opened my eyes, I saw him. My old piano teacher. He was sitting there next to one of his students, who I recognised as the boy who used to have his lessons just after mine. My stomach lurched, but I couldn't pinpoint what emotion I was experiencing. Fear? Hatred? Disbelief? Why was he here? Memories came gushing back. I didn't want him here, spoiling my night.

He recognised me. It had been years since we had last met. It had been a negative final lesson. He had told me I was no good anyway, so teaching me was a waste of time. He smiled at me now. But somehow, he too seemed unsure how to react. He looked older now, frailer. I looked at his student's fingers. Were they raw and sore as well? No, not really.

He asked me what I was playing. I answered, but all the while I wanted to run away. I heard the applause as the child on stage finished her piece. I heard my name being announced through the speaker in the greenroom. I gathered my music sheets and left, knees shaking.

I had to do it. Now my performance had to be perfect, not just for me or for the audience, but to put right all the accusations laid against me. For my sore knuckles and torn books. For those pair of ears in the green room to listen and take back his hurtful words. There was a lot at stake when I placed my fingers on the keyboard.

Softly, I began. My most beloved piece of music. I halted at every pause and raced through every run and trill. Adagio. Pianissimo. Allegro. I was lost within the fantasy created by Mozart.

When I stopped, there was silence in the hall. Then, thunderous applause. I curtseyed, not registering the response. My mind was blank. I couldn't believe that my fingers had created such magic. I couldn't believe that I had actually been there on the stage and performed. I stepped back into the green room.

He was still there. I felt like an eight-year-old again, running back to my teacher, waiting for words of praise or admonishment. I gathered up my bag and books, and tried to ignore him.

My head was throbbing and I was afraid I'd pass out if I didn't leave the green room quickly enough.

'You were very good,' he said, finally. His voice was softer than I had imagined.

'Thank you,' I replied, and glanced quickly towards him.

'Very good,' he said softly and then busied himself with his student. I left the green room and walked out into the courtyard. The cool breeze hit me and I smiled. I noticed that I was lighter on my feet. I felt like I was shedding old skin.

He said I was good. It didn't really matter so much now.

It mattered so much to me. ◼

When They Took All the Trees

by Charlie J. Stephens

The kitchen chair where I usually sat for more serious conversations was covered in worn upholstery with small blue birds on it. I traced the outlines of the wings with my finger as Mom talked, letting the weight of her question sink in. I was eight years old.

I told her honestly that no, I did not remember.

I remembered X though, someone Mom dated on and off when we lived in that little yellow house with the crooked front steps. He was from a nearby tribe and had once tried to teach me traditional beading, but my small hands couldn't get the needle through the leather. Mom defended me that afternoon, telling him that five-year-olds can't really do things like that yet. I can still feel the shame of being a disappointment. What made it worse was all those tiny glass beads scattering across the floor when he knocked the piece of leather out of my hands and stormed off.

X stands out for other reasons too. One time I went to the hallway late at night and peered around the door at the moment his massive arm swung out and smashed into the side of Mom's face. In slow motion I watched her head turn at a strange angle as splatters of blood hit the wall behind her.

I attacked him, screaming and punching, but I was too small, too light, too inconsequential. After that, for months and years, sometimes when I closed my eyes I saw those red dots against the white wall like so much violent confetti.

I started having a recurring nightmare then, of crouching behind the hedge in our yard and shooting any men who tried to get near us. In my dreams I mostly missed, and they just kept coming up the middle of the street like so many comic book zombies.

The beating wasn't enough for Mom to break up with X, but what happened to me was. She was willing to go over the story as many times as I needed. It was something I kept returning to – trying to make sense of it through the retelling.

Mom told me that she had needed something from the store, and left me with X. When she came back sooner than expected, having forgotten her wallet, the door to the bathroom was already locked with me and X inside. Though she banged on the door, growing more frantic with each quiet second, it took a long time for him to open it. She told me she knew immediately that something was wrong, that I was pale and clammy, and I wouldn't speak. She didn't tell me if she inspected my genitals for harm, but she must have. I imagine her gently putting me in the bath with bubbles like she often did, a rubber ducky I had named Ernie bobbing along beside me, while she stroked my hair and told me it was going to be OK.

For years after that I really only spoke to Mom, my grandma, and my best friend, a neighbor's kid whose dad had a broken jaw and ate blended-up hamburgers through a straw. Mom didn't press charges. It was the late 70s. She thought that no one would believe her and she was really worried that in the end I'd somehow be taken away from her. Those years are filled with sharp images. I studied each one like a dissociated psychologist, trying to understand something new about these humans around me from a vast distance.

Learning about my assault felt abstract, but still something to consider. In my teenage years I wondered if or how it had influenced me. After the incident I presented as increasingly androgynous, but maybe that was already part of my path. I liked existing in the middle, played on boys' sports teams, wore western shirts with their pearl snaps, cut my hair short with my grandma's sewing scissors. Being androgynous felt like freedom, like I had an uncharted world open to me that pushed beyond what anyone expected from a 'girl' or 'boy' at the time. The rules didn't apply to me, and I felt relief and freedom there, uncategorized.

It wasn't until my twenties and the arrival of the internet that I looked X up and, not really expecting to find him, found him.

I learned that he'd been sent to the Children's Farm Home as a child when big timber companies had pushed in, took all the trees, filled the rivers with silt, killed off the salmon runs, destroyed the livelihoods – and lives – of his parents and community. For the next five years, X was severely abused at Children's Farm Home. Old pictures of the building show a stately red and white plantation-style house on 300 acres, but there still wasn't anywhere for scared boys to hide.

William Dufort, since convicted, had worked there since the 60s. His specialty was sodomy. For decades he abused boys, all sent there from the dire circumstances of broken, institutionalized, imprisoned or dead parents. During the trial it came out that Dufort had all the boys' files marked in a color-coded system denoting which ones sexually aroused him.

In the years after his time in our home, X grew up, made it back to his tribe, had a family, became an activist. He shed the fetid stain of whiteness, taught his children traditional ways, became a Sundancer, grew old. One of the last things I found was a song X recorded. In it, he sounds beautiful and healed, singing about spirits and a favorite auntie. I still listen to it sometimes when I'm alone.

The song is a thread of sound connecting back to our shared history, but without any of the violence attached. Colonization ripped through our little yellow house back then, and we all still somehow made it through that long, painful quiet—

     each of us finding our own salved voices.   ∎

The Royal Society of Literature

RSL MEMBERSHIP
JOIN NOW

GILLIAN ANDERSON & ANDREW O'HAGAN

- **FREE TICKETS** TO IN-PERSON AND ONLINE EVENTS
- OUR QUARTERLY NEWSPAPER, *OUR MUTUAL FRIEND*
- **FREE SUBSCRIPTION** TO THE *RSL REVIEW* MAGAZINE
- **SPECIAL OFFERS** FROM OUR WONDERFUL PARTNERS ACROSS **THEATRE, FILM AND ALL THINGS LITERARY**

ALL OF THIS COULD BE YOURS,
WITH **MEMBERSHIP STARTING AT JUST**
£40 FOR A WHOLE YEAR

NEIL GAIMAN & MARLON JAMES

BE PART OF THE ACTION
DIGITAL EVENTS PASS

WHEREVER YOU ARE, **GET INVOLVED IN OUR STELLAR EVENTS PROGRAMME** BY SNAPPING UP AN RSL DIGITAL EVENTS PASS TODAY

ALL OF OUR EVENTS ARE **AVAILABLE ONLINE FOR JUST £25 A YEAR** SO YOU WON'T MISS A THING

JOIN NOW

what I saw

will

not be

what I see

by Anna Vaught

'Know then, that the world exists for you.
For you is the phenomenon perfect.
What we are, that only can we see.'
— Ralph Waldo Emerson, *Nature*

The trouble with trauma is that it's *very* persistent. If you are extremely young or your self-belief has been eviscerated, you may not know that you are experiencing it. You may doubt the veracity of your own perception, or perhaps worst of all, you may think it is all you deserve. Then, however well-meaning it might be, people who were there or nearby may tell you that you imagined it, or the ideas were put in your head by someone else, or perhaps, that if it had happened, they would have known. You may try to discuss things with those closest to you and instead of listening, they gently push your words away, swat you towards a particular position: the strange child, the outlier, loved but unreliable and with a heated imagination; a sense of drama. If you put together all the things I describe, then you have a situation in which you cannot tell your story. In your darkest moments you doubt yourself but are reminded that it would not be believable for you to make up a visceral and multi-sensory response, sudden and unbidden, from a story you invented. This is what trauma does to you: complex and extended trauma within a family home, of violence, gaslighting, a stark and inappropriate eroticism – all bound up with lovely things, so your head spins and you would be prepared to forgive now, as an adult, because of the kindnesses and the lovely things, had one person ever believed how you were and what you felt; had you not had to work at it for decades: staying well, learning to trust people and your own narrative.

If one person had said sorry. Or I ought to have believed you.

Then, without a great push of mind clearing and determination, a tree could be just a tree.

Let me explain, as I once had to for a therapist. I told how I had always loved the natural world and all I could see in it. When trauma has impacted on you, it is very difficult to see things freshly; they are frequently subsumed by nostalgia of a most uncomfortable kind and, for me, involving a radical pull on all my senses. It was important for me to look at a tree and see only a tree; any outing my imagination wished to make would be artless and new.

'But at the end of the day, a tree is only a tree,' the therapist said.

And I said, '*Except it is not.* A tree is also a collocation of impressions and memories; smells and the texture on my tongue and so much more: it is the vivacity of memory, punching me, unbidden, from the ur-tree, something I must have looked at or been with in a time of early fear or need. That

Everything is loaded with nostalgia, dripping with it in a way that is tiresome and enervating

tree informed all subsequent trees.'

I explained that all my life, I had been observing the things I loved and wanted to know in the natural world. I am still like that. I grew up very rurally, between Somerset, West Wiltshire and Southwest Wales, the three places I know and love best, and I would roam and escape as often as possible. Out of stress, but also adventure and joy. I told the therapist that it had always been a challenge for me to see things freshly and this had been a lifetime job of work, but I also took time to tell her some of the joyous detail I had been able to observe, examples of which I will outline later.

First, though, let me explain more of what I mean by a painful nostalgia. One of the vagaries of a lively psychiatric history such as mine is that you may, apparently without choice, baulk at living in the moment. Everything is loaded with nostalgia, dripping with it in a way that is tiresome

and enervating: you can't see the live oak for the
Spanish moss and boy do you hate that moss,
tumbling down and catching your shoulder in the
breeze. And the nostalgia is not kind. You look at
a shimmering Christmas bauble and yet you see
another pretty Christmas bauble of times past.
Its prettiness – fugged with the familiar scents of
cinnamon and cloves and all the season's spice –
will soon have you tensing your muscles as you
remember the underside of the caroling and the
wassail: you knew you weren't wanted and you
swallowed up the curses; you went into your room,
having been told you didn't deserve the presents,
and you longed to expire, immolated in your fit
of self-loathing. You let people who bore you gifts
do the most appalling things to you and didn't tell
anyone until you fell apart altogether and at that
point, someone had to help because you had three
children who were dependent on you. I know it was
just a silly bauble, but some minds work like that,
skipping from thought to thought and unable to see
something, just now, for what it is. I can tell you
that, over the years, I have experienced delirium
over pickles, torments over toffees, cabbage,
gooseberries, spotted dick, caravans and those lines
in Dylan Thomas that tell (in my imagination) of
a picture or a shroud saying, "Thou shalt not" –
oh yes. These were things I saw: in sweetie shops
where mother pinched my hand and I tried to rock
shut, away from her; in intense vegetable-boiling
kitchens, through spat kindness, at funerals and in
beastly, vaporous dark pantries. "Thou shalt not"

hung in my paternal grandmother's house: once, with typical incongruity, above a picture of blue-tinged kittens playing with wool; and, again, below a depiction of a particularly dark and evil dead aunt, whose scorn slid down the wall and onto the sateen cushions below. From both shalt-nots, spoke out a dry, thin voice: "Thou shalt not" cry or laugh; "Thou shalt not" spare the nasty little child. "Thou shalt not" tell your story because who would listen to *you*? And the thin dry voice spoke to a little girl. She was me and I was so, so scared.

And what is more, there was a beautiful old Victoria plum tree outside; there were staked dahlias and deep grass full of clover and, beyond, I knew there were early purple orchids and if I had walked on, I would have seen harebells. And all would have limned with a story and a feeling I did not want them to have, and the mind going rat-a-tat-tat and everything shining and confusing. Now do you see why a tree is not just a tree to me? Or at least, what my challenge was in viewing the world around me? I have been determined though, to see and to observe in detail, so I am going to outline some favourite things for you. Some plants, a tree.

Let us begin with a very ordinary and ubiquitous miracle: rosebay willowherb. Rosebay – my willowherb of choice – which, with its full and fuchsia family, must often go unnoticed. Have you ever looked at the plant and spent time with it, observing it as the plant bursts open and delicate filigree webbing holds seeds that blow out into the world? Cotton and gossamer; magic. Varieties are

everywhere and I venerate them: by the side of the
M4 motorway, by the least promising layby on the
A55, and in the past on a rough and tumble bank
in Somerset, where I grew up. I knew, even as a
small child, from my *Collins Complete Guide to British
Wildlife*, that willowherb had a rough and tumble
family too. There is the New Zealand willowherb,
a latter-day interloper, marsh, great, broad leaf
(the most common) and square stemmed. In my
experience, a lot of people do not seem to know
what they are called, though they recognise them,
seeing them only as weeds or a sort of pretender
to foxglove. The rosebay was always my favourite
because of its lovely name and the play of syllables
seemed particularly pretty, and because on the
rough and tumble bank, it was abundant and
I loved the filigree and cotton and would come
in covered with the stuff, racing to get it off my
clothes. I would hide amongst those stiffly erect
stems and unequal petals, and wonder at how fine
the name sounded in Latin. Say it aloud, trippingly
on your tongue: *Epilobium angustifolium*. I believe
my maternal grandmother called it fireweed and
my father said you could not kill it − exactly what I

I loved the filigree and cotton and would come in covered with the stuff, racing to get it off my clothes

liked about it. It thrived.

I know that once I would look at it, as I do
now, and try to enter the vibrancy of that fire. I
remember the bank at home, full of it, bold and

scruffy; I remember, as if I were living it now, that I tried to look at it and make a new world or find something with which to communicate, but I did not know what. The fireweed description stuck though, because I thought of the plant as both beautiful and angry; resilient, in a way I was not yet, but hoped to be. It reveled in its untidy smudges on the rough and tumble bank, and I knew it would come back again and again; I knew I would see it thrive everywhere I looked. A piercing memory erupts each time I think of it: this is about another bank, a long one underneath a laundry line on the edge of an orchard where I went on my third birthday. I have always been told that I could not possibly remember this birthday, but I can feel and see it vividly and I know I was wearing pink and looking at yellow and together, pink and yellow, we were the colour of rhubarb and custard sweets. The faces of the celandines opened to the sun. That small girl was standing on a soft bank in a spring breeze as the laundry blew high above her there in the orchard. The breeze blew cold, but there were currents of warmth about her legs as the day decided whether it would whip or kiss. Sitting now, legs akimbo on the bank, that little girl who was me saw the faces of the yellow celandines open to the sun, the hedge full of primroses beyond the whirling laundry.

She was happy.

Just as she was bathed in hope and fire by the rosebay willowherb, here was more bathing: she knew that she could bury her face in the violet patch and lounge there with their sweetness. That is, for a short while, because this child always knew that after such delicacy came danger and threat and there was no one to tell. But if you know that the faces of the celandines open to the sun, time and again, and the willowherb rebels however much you tidy and cut, there is an angry power to that, felt

It was always a sign, for me... of something blessedly important, familiar, immortal and a haven for bees

even by a small child.

This plant comforts me now, as it did throughout my childhood and teenage years. You could be near it almost anywhere; it always came back if you mowed it, scythed it or tried to destroy and sterilise the ground around it. It was always a sign, for me, not of a weed, a not important plant, but of something blessedly important, familiar, immortal and a haven for bees – there are few things I like more than bees. If, as a child, you are surrounded by a sort of passionate morbidity, by frightening psychiatric incidents in the family – frightening because it is spoken of behind closed doors and with euphemism – it may be that you need to latch on to things around you which provide stability and reassurance. Much of this was in the natural world for me, often accompanied with a book.

Now let me tell you about a significant tree. In the long and straggling wood attached to our house, there was a tree, and this was a tree I have always loved. I loved all trees, but this appeared to have a particularly strong personality and something within it which offered comfort. It was a beech tree. The Woodland Trust has this to say about the common beech, which is anything but common: 'Monumental, majestic, home to rare wildlife. Beech is an enchanting species and known as the queen of British trees. To wander beneath the leafy canopy, its cathedral-like branches spreading

...as I whispered to the beech, the beech whispered to its cousins and, perhaps, shared my whispers, and I was less alone

upwards, is an awe-inspiring experience.' All of this. *Fagus sylvatica*, my *Fagus sylvatica*, had a smooth bark I would hold my cheek against, lukewarm and giving. It had a kind of firm foot, to one side, where the trunk curved out into the soil, so there was a gentle child-sized slope to stand on; from my purchase here, I would climb onto the tree and wrap my arms around it tightly. I would whisper to the tree and make a wish, which usually involved being a long way away, or being in this beautiful place, but feeling safe. If I wished to think hard about travel, well I had already stepped aboard the tree, slightly above the earth, so my imagination needed only take a short step before we were airborne, flying to families of beech all over the world. Perhaps the demurer *Fagus grandifolia* in North America, the small American beech. I had looked them all up, inventing a family for my own beech and thinking that, as I whispered to the beech, the beech whispered to its cousins and, perhaps, shared my whispers, and I was less alone.

Frequently, I did not feel safe, growing up. Even writing this, I do not feel safe because those feelings ebb back. One of the things that long and complex trauma has done to me – and in the context of my story not being believed – is that I often feel there is imminent danger, however much I know, rationally, that this is not the case. As far as I understand it, I have developed around an uncertain core. So, while I have done my best, with latter-day therapeutic support, to bed in new ideas, if my senses taste something bitterly familiar, back it floods in. This is a time where an intimate encounter with plants or natural phenomena are a salve, speaking a language which is safe and true. There is more, because just as I look at the bold fuchsia of the rosebay willowherb and feel a lift in my spirits, I sometimes see the forms of the natural world as metaphor for something larger and so much better. Each striation or delicate whimsy in a plant is like a word or an idea. I cannot read it, but metaphor may connote something we can only begin to grasp at, numinous and redolent of such hope. Fireweed; fuchsia: intemperate straggling plant. What might it say, if one day I understood? What of the solidity of the beech tree and, if I concentrated very hard, the delicate fluctuations in texture, temperature even (I was so certain I felt it, like a pulse!). What if it told of clues to a greater and everlasting wood and this place was my church? That is how I feel around trees and, were I to go into an old church, I feel as much pull of faith in the moss and lichen of a wall as kneeling by an altar cloth.

I have always walked out and loved it, and my favourite place is the Pembrokeshire Coast Path. I walked a section recently, out at St David's Head, beginning near St Non's and the statue of Our Lady and the lovely little well at her feet. It was the finest of days, but when I set out, I felt that pull of nostalgia. My late father and I would walk, in stretches, the whole of the Pembrokeshire Coast Path. The coastline holds memories, both troubling and beautiful, of St Bride's Bay on a fine day and setting out on a voyage with my father. Up and down, climbing over the rocks; sometimes – or at least this is how it was remembered – perilously close to the cliff edge, or along thickets of gnarled, lichen-covered trees. We did a different stage each day. I climbed on rocks at the water's edge, took the wave in my face, coming up new for a while and chewing on bladderwrack seaweed. The cormorants eyed me suspiciously, sleek and stretching out their wet wings to sun and breeze. Out there in the bay, I could see the great tankers waiting to come into Pembroke Dock or Milford Haven, or perhaps they were setting out for balmy climes.

My father was then, as he is now, incomplete; shadowy, an unknowable figure. I can tell you everything about his accomplishments and his hobbies and about how hard he worked though, so that had to be knowing enough. He was a silent man, but a teacher, woodsmith and wordsmith; creator of fires; fine cricketer; lay preacher: many lives in one. He had survived the dark peculiarities of his own family home, was mad for petrol lawnmowers with their craft and their finely calibrated maintenance, chainsaws and the correct manner of cleaving logs (done with mathematical precision), a skill I still love and try to observe, because it's still beauty and still magic, even if it came from the wrong hands. So, who he was, the man who was my father, I did not really know. As we walked, I tried to talk to him about thrift, seabirds or whether the cormorants that had scrutinised me on the rocks could be trained to dive down and fish and come back up and drop their catch, like I had read they were in China or Southern India. And once, particularly daring, but really against my better judgement, I sucked hard at the coconut nectar from the gorse flowers that ranked the coast path in abundance and asked him A Difficult Question. I said, knowing that my parents spoke so highly of Number One Son – of how easy and gentle he was, while I stayed an eldritch child: 'Dad, can I ask you something? I want...for you to tell me something?'

'Oh! What is it now?' The watery grey-granite eyes looked past me.

'I think I want some reassurance. I mean, I'm sorry, I mean that I know Mum doesn't like me and that I am a trial.'

'Quickly, get on with it. I want to identify those birds on the rock there and can't if you keep talking.'

'Well, when you talk about me, do you say that I'm, that I'm, well, OK?'

His answer was blunt. 'We prefer to spend time with Number One Son. He listens to us; he likes to be with us, and he never says a word. And you should know you are here under sufferance. Now pass me the bird spotter.'

'But I listen. It's how I know you like cormorants and thrift and gorse nectar.'

'You are talking.'

'Dad, I want to talk to you.'

■ '*He* never says a word. *You* are always talking.'

'Be quiet, you little cuss.'

I know that I sucked harder on the gorse nectar and that I wanted to die, right then; even assessed a trajectory off the cliff. I did not jump. Instead, I passed him the bird spotter and always remembered this conversation. And I would remember the advice I overheard him giving to parents, with: 'Never crush a child's spirit' being an important phrase. But the sufferance, the plainly preferred sibling, the palpable disappointment in and plain dislike of the daughter; it rankled on the clearest day: '*He* never says a word. *You* are always talking.' I couldn't keep quiet because the words were so beautiful, whatever risks they brought with them. And I couldn't keep quiet because the world and all that was in it was so beautiful, how could I have done? But, always and innocently, there breathed the syntax of damnation at my back and in my ear. Now there was a challenge to suck gorse nectar as if for the first time; to see that saffron rush as if for the first time and feel the velvet of its petals, without a shudder. **H**

Material from this essay will be published in Anna Vaught's memoir, These Envoys of Beauty, *forthcoming in Spring 2023 from Reflex Press. www.reflex.press/these-envoys-of-beauty-by-anna-vaught/*

ilerhouse.press

OUT NOW

BOILER HOUSE PRESS

Speaking

in Tongues

by S.Y. Tam

The retired sign language interpreter sat by my side in the car. He was 65, with mild gray eyes encased behind filmy glasses, and his slender fingers punctuated his speech as he introduced himself. He told me he lived in Texas with his wife and children, who had stayed behind. It was his fourth year attending the North American Esperanto Congress, and now when he saw the familiar green highway sign – RALEIGH, 55 miles – a thrill of excitement ran through his veins. Like coming home, he breathed. It's like coming home.

I laughed, intrigued by his language of homecoming. I remarked that there was something strange and sweet about his nostalgia for a place he visited only once a year.

He smiled and asked me if I knew the story of *Brigadoon,* about a mysterious village in the Scottish countryside that only appeared one day a year. There was a love story connected with it, he said, but the real romance was the fleeting chance to trade the familiar for the faerie. The village was enchanted and idyllic, its harmony preserved forever. Their summer Esperanto gatherings were a little like that, he explained. A brief, sweet reunion – yes, sweet was a good word for it – that evaporated with the morning mist, and then returned them to their ordinary lives and families.

We rode in silence, the last of the sunlight slanting across the freeway. My companion tapped my shoulder amiably. And do you know, he said, if I were in a group of strangers and one of them was an Esperantist, I would give my wallet to her in full confidence that when I asked for it back, not a dollar – not a single coin – would be out of place. He raised a playful finger, leaning close. You wonder why? Well, that is what you must discover for yourself this weekend.

I asked him if his wife or children spoke the language, and he said they did not. Though they were supportive, they did not really understand his interest in Esperanto. Most Esperantists, he confessed, did not share the language with their families.

As we coasted along placid suburban streets with brick houses and flower beds, the interpreter shared that Esperantists often learned the language on their own, through the different and meandering waterways of life. Some were idealists, in love with the romance of the forgotten language and its ideology of world peace; others were linguaphiles, interested in the syntax of history's most successful invented language. Together, they formed their own kind of family across the world: odd-ones-out learning the largely unused language.

And you? he turned to ask. Where do you come from?

I started, then realized he was asking about my interest in Esperanto. I am reporting for New York Public Radio, I replied. I'm doing a piece on language politics. This was entirely true, but I was conscious of a strained note in my voice: neutral, evasive. I do not speak the language, I added. I'm trying to find out why millions of people choose to learn Esperanto today.

Very good. He looked pleased. Esperanto requires an open mind – but even more, an open heart. I listen to NPR all the time; it has great, unbiased reporting.

The interpreter laughed at my startled reaction. You were caught up in the dream of Esperanto, he teased

I said nothing, retreating further into myself.

A crunch of gravel marked our arrival at William Peace University. The interpreter laughed at my startled reaction. You were caught up in the dream of Esperanto, he teased. Well, here we are. He opened the door for me, and I stepped out into the summer evening. The sun had set, but its heat still infused the air. Other attendees were milling about the lawn. My companion pointed out the 'Old Guard,' a cluster of elderly Esperantists, mostly men; there was also a scattering of participants in their twenties and thirties, sporting totes emblazoned with the Green Star. I noted the group was mostly white. Ah, yes, the interpreter said, shifting his weight uncomfortably. We usually have more Latin Americans, many international attendees. But for reasons you can imagine, this year we have almost none. Only a couple of participants from Brazil and Canada.

I could indeed imagine. It was the summer after Trump's election. The past year's chants, rallies, and media frenzy still echoed in my sleepless nights. But I just nodded; I had other reasons for being interested in the congress that year, which I was not about to disclose to a stranger.

A stout-bellied man with a lobster dangling from his lanyard greeted my companion with a shout, and the interpreter was encircled by other congress returnees. I glimpsed the dark contours of a colonnade at the end of a tree-lined walkway, and quietly found my way to registration.

With estimates ranging widely from one hundred thousand to two million speakers, Esperanto is the most historically successful 'constructed language.' About one thousand people are native speakers, who grow up in Esperanto-speaking families, but most speak their region's languages for communication with their broader community. The language was invented in 1887 by a Jewish-Polish eye doctor, Dr Ludovik Lazarus Zamenhof. It has survived two world wars and now spans over a hundred countries, mostly in Europe, East Asia, and South America.

Esperanto means 'the hopeful one.'[1] Both pragmatic and idealistic, Zamenhof first published

---

1 The O.E.D. traces the etymology of the word Esperanto to the penname of its inventor on his 1887 book, 'Dr. Esperanto,' from the Esperantic verb *esperi* ('to hope'), presumably related to the Latin *sperare* ('to hope'), i.e. literally, 'Dr. Hoping-one.'

the language manifesto under the pseudonym *Doktoro Esperanto* (Doctor Hopeful). He wanted his language to be easy to learn for everyone, despite its Indo-European origin and influences. Esperanto is constructed from a simplified grammar (no gendered subjects, minimal conjugations; all adjectives end in 'a', all nouns in 'o') and basic vocabulary of 900 root words. Indeed, one study among Francophone children found it 10 times faster to learn than English, Italian, and German.

But behind these humble linguistic Lego blocks lay a vast vision. 'La interna ideo de Esperanto,' Zamenhof declared in 1912, 'estas sur neŭtrala lingva fundamento.' The core idea of Esperanto was to build a neutral linguistic foundation that would eliminate national borders in favor of universal brotherhood: it was intended to create world peace through perfect communication. The global establishment of this *interna ideo* would be the *fina venko* – the final victory.

The Oxford English Dictionary defines 'constructed language' in opposition to a 'natural language,' which 'has evolved naturally, as distinguished from an artificial language devised for international communications or for formal logical or mathematical purposes.' But the opposition between 'constructed' and 'natural' language is slightly misleading. After all, every language is constructed, composed of sounds and strokes that express our coordinates of reality. But all these building blocks come naturally to humans: babies usually begin babbling by six months, and the mastery of language is generally complete by age eight. Language acquisition is interwoven into the fabric of our species, and our complexity of language is part of what makes humans special.

According to linguist John McWhorter, we are the only species that can imagine worlds that we ourselves have never seen, with statements such as, 'I've seen the carcass of a giant squid washed up on a beach missing an eye.' There are many theories for how our language evolved such possibility, such a scope for symbols – that speech started as song, or whistles warning of predators. Most likely, language evolved out of the need to coordinate the scavenging of large mammals, such as mammoths, and other feats of collaboration that humans had no hope of accomplishing on their own.

Most likely, language evolved out of the need to coordinate the scavenging of large mammals, such as mammoths

Still other stories speak of how language is not only composed of symbols, but also is itself an existential symbol for human connection. These narratives characterize the problem of language as one of misunderstanding: the eternal slippage between what we mean and say, and what others hear and understand.

The Babel story in Genesis, the first book of the Torah, recounts how humans lost the ability to understand each other. In it, men seek to build a tower that reaches the heavens: a rebellion of cosmic dimensions. To stop them, God scatters them into many nations and tongues across the Earth. 'That is why it was called Babel, because there the Lord confused the language of the whole world.'[2] Judaic scholar Esther Schor points out in an interview with *Freakonomics* that the Babel story can also be read as the origin myth of nation-states and ethnic division: Babel directly follows the Table of Nations, as though the Genesis author were tracing the birth of our political borders back to the beginning of linguistic diversity.

Judaic scholar Esther Schor pointed out ... that the Babel story can also be read as the origin myth of nation-states and ethnic division

Growing up Jewish in anti-Semitic Poland, Zamenhof also tracked his experiences of ethnic strife to the confusion of tongues in his neighborhood. 'In Białystok, the inhabitants were divided into four distinct elements: Russians, Poles, Germans and Jews; each of these spoke their own language and looked on all the others as enemies,' he wrote in an 1895 letter. 'In such a town, a sensitive nature feels more acutely than elsewhere the misery caused by language division and sees at every step that the diversity of languages is the first, or at least the most influential, basis for the separation of the human family into groups of

---

2 Genesis 11:9 (NIV). Schor points out in her book, *Bridge of Words: Esperanto and the Dream of a Universal Language*, that there are various interpretations among scholars about the nature of this linguistic punishment. From the Middle Ages onward, the Babel story was proverbially referred to as 'the confusion of tongues' (*confusio linguarum*), suggesting a multiplication of languages. However, the original Hebrew word for 'language' (*safah*) is always singular in the text, implying misunderstanding among speakers of the same language.

enemies.' He became convinced that a universal language could provide the solution to the problems that ravaged Europe: the rising nationalism, anti-Semitism, and the creation of nation-states that would bring about the first of two world wars less than twenty years later.

On the second day of the Esperanto congress, I set up my equipment to conduct interviews in the black box theater on campus. I had announced the night before that I was looking for willing Esperantists to be interviewed for public radio, and by lunchtime there was a steady trickle arriving to share their experiences. The theater was a musty, square room whose floor-to-ceiling black was designed to create a flexible performance space, but also produced a sense of temporal dislocation after hours of interviews. Stories blurred, then overlapped: Americans and Canadians who traveled the world, hosted for free by fellow Esperantists because of their shared language.

Joel and Ĵenja were the last to appear. They had been married over a decade, and Esperanto lay at the heart of their romance. As they sat down, I informed them we were on the record: our entire conversation was being recorded and could be used for broadcast. I directed my microphone at Ĵenja first, asking her how the two of them met.

She leaned forward, her thin hair falling around her pale face. 'We met during the Cold War,' she said, her voice soft and sibilant. 'I hired him to help me edit an international Esperanto magazine. We knew each other first through letters, because I'm from Ukraine, and he's American.'

'A small-town boy,' Joel chuckled. His wire-rimmed glasses reflected two oblongs of light as he hulked towards the microphone. 'I was a small-town boy from Georgia. Esperanto changed my life. I might still be in Georgia, not having traveled or anything like that, if I hadn't come across Esperanto in a bookstore as a teen. I was always an odd kid, into encyclopedias and languages.'

Joel spoke in urgent bursts, his shoulders slouched self-consciously into his heavy torso. A portrait of him as a teenager began to emerge in my mind: hiding in the library from football jocks who mocked him for learning Latin, overhearing gossip against the González girls and their closeted brother. 'I could have been like my schoolmates. But the first Esperanto speaker I met was gay; Esperanto opened my mind, threw me into contact with people I'd never have talked to. And just, when I see what's happening with Trump, Mexico… sorry, I don't mean to get political. But without Esperanto, I might not have traveled – certainly wouldn't have married a communist!'

'Well, we both grew up thinking of the other side as the enemy.' Ĵenja smiled. 'We wouldn't have met without Esperanto. It's not just the language; it's like a value system. There are so few of us in each country, we always connect across borders. He came to visit me, eventually; we traveled, fell in love. The rest is, as they say, history.'

Their knees bent tightly towards each other, and for a moment I could see them. The Cold

War couple. The slender Ukrainian and broad-shouldered American, speaking across the East and West divide in their own special tongue on the cobbled streets of old European cities.

The slender Ukrainian and broad-shouldered American, speaking across the East and West divide in their own special tongue on the cobbled streets of old European cities

'For me, Esperanto's kind of like – I apologize, I'm a theologian, so the word I would use is "realized eschatology."' Joel's fist clenched on his knee, a blotchy flush along his cheeks. 'I know it sounds almost evangelical to talk about it like that, but I believe it. What we have in the Esperanto community is a microcosm of what could be, should be. This community that spans languages, religions, races – on a small scale, it's the world Zamenhof dreamed of.'

His forehead shone with sweat, his eyes earnestly fixed on mine. He looked so sincere that I suspended my skepticism. I allowed myself to lose track of time, drawn along by the theologian's epic thread. The black box theater became the stage on which their love story about language transmuted into a struggle for our nation's soul. I was reminded of the Pentecost story in the New Testament, recounted in the book of Acts. After Jesus's ascension, the Holy Spirit descends on the disciples, resting over them as tongues of fire. The disciples are enabled by the Spirit to 'speak in tongues,' astounding the God-fearing Jews who assemble before them from every nation under heaven. Each one is utterly amazed to hear their own language being spoken. 'Aren't all these who are speaking Galileans?' they exclaim. 'Then how is it that each of us hears them in our native language? Parthians, Medes and Elamites … Cretans and Arabs – we hear them declaring the wonders of God in our own tongues!' If Babel is an origin story of how misunderstanding was born, then Pentecost is a vision of understanding restored. For Joel, Esperanto was this realized eschatology: a world in which he was no longer lost in translation.

... even within nations, within the same language, we grew increasingly deaf to each other as we shouted louder and louder

The red light on my recorder blinked. The memory was full; it was almost midnight. I thanked them for their time, gathered my equipment, and slowly walked across the campus. A fragrant breeze nudged me, and I paused to listen to the enveloping chorus of crickets. It was hard to imagine that just two days before, I had left my office to barrel through crowds on my way to the airport, the roar of planes ripping open the New York skyline. Everything about that morning seemed a lifetime away.

I went to bed but couldn't sleep. Joel's words flickered around my mind; a moth beat itself against the window. Alone in my room, my cheeks grew wet. Hearing the theologian pour forth about Esperanto, I couldn't help but think that its project seemed as improbable as ever, with the rise of isolationist nationalism in Europe and America. In

Zamenhof's bid to unite the world through language, he seemed to believe that linguistic communication led to global community. But in my experience of the now English-dominated world, shared language did not lead to shared understanding. Just the previous year, the United Kingdom had voted to leave the European Union, which had been founded to protect against the extreme nationalism that devastated the continent during the world wars. A few months later, the United States had elected a president who partly campaigned on building a wall to keep out Mexicans. Both events were wildly polarizing, and even within nations, within the same language, we grew increasingly deaf to each other as we shouted louder and louder.

I was reminded, too, of a global encounter with English – a language whose promises I had for a time believed. During my time as a graduate student in England, I had boarded a bus in Oxford and requested a single trip to Littlemore. The bus driver printed me the wrong ticket, and the return fare flashed up. I pointed out the mistake, and he stared at me impatiently. I already printed the ticket, he said, jabbing at the console. Return to Littlemore.

Right, yes, I said, but the problem is that's not what I asked for.

The problem is, he corrected, you can't speak English properly.

We stared at each other. His pale blue eyes narrowed at my wide dark ones. I stood stunned, my response reduced by shock to the rudimentary: but I can – I certainly *can* speak English.

He rolled his eyes, printed a single fare, and waved me to the back. I spent the rest of the ride – after taking down the bus number to make an official complaint later, which was eventually dismissed as 'unsubstantiated'[3] – in a spiral of humiliation at what had not been said, at what I wished or should have said. I suddenly understood why my mother had become a snob after she immigrated from Hong Kong to America. To this day, she steeled herself against barbs about her 'bad English' by flaunting her U.C. Berkeley degree — she had graduated from one of the most competitive state universities in the country — which I had always felt to be in poor taste. But there I was, my mother's daughter, standing before the bus driver. I had arrived to complete a master's degree in English literature on a prestigious academic scholarship at Oxford University. As I burned under the driver's scornful gaze, I held between us my degree and bitterly wanted to point out the irony that, of all things, he had picked on my mastery of the English language. It was only later, after the shame had subsided, that I appreciated the real irony: as we each clung to our separate enclaves of exclusivity – race, nationality, education – English was the only thing in common between us.

---

3 My complaint of racial harassment was dismissed as follows: 'due to a faulty hard-drive, the C.C.T.V. footage of the incident was not available to view and as such, your allegation was deemed as unsubstantiated.' I was assured in response to my follow-up email that 'the appropriate actions will be taken.' What these were, however, I would not be told even after a third attempt: 'As stated, Employment Law prevents us from disclosing the exact actions taken against the driver.'

With an estimated 1.5 billion speakers, English is an indisputably global language: today's *lingua franca*.[4] Those numbers are particularly impressive, when considering that less than 40 percent of those are native speakers. (Compare this to Mandarin, which also has over one billion speakers, but only about 20 percent are non-native speakers.) Like Esperanto,

> **Unlike Esperanto, which is mostly learned through free online resources today, English language education constitutes a lucrative industry**

the majority of speakers learn English in addition to their mother tongue. Unlike Esperanto, which is mostly learned through free online resources today, English language education constitutes a lucrative industry, particularly in the United States and the United Kingdom. Economist François Grin estimated that the United Kingdom alone gained around €17 billion annually – about one percent of its gross national product – from the dominance of English in 2005. This revenue stemmed partly from the United Kingdom's thriving English-language teaching industry drawing foreign learners, and the comparative absence of its own foreign language costs (native English speakers being less likely to learn foreign languages).

We live in an era of unprecedented globalization, but not one that has been brought about through an ophthalmologist's egalitarian dream of world peace.

---

4 Lingua franca, literally 'Frankish tongue,' is a term whose seventeenth century Italian origins trace the ever-shifting contours of linguistic dominance. Lingua franca was a pidgin language with roots in southern Romance languages and used for trading purpose cross the Mediterranean, northern Africa, and the Middle East.

The spread of English can be largely credited to the colonial conquests of the British Empire, which at its height held about 25 percent of the world's population and land mass under its sway. The subsequent rise of the American economy, military, and higher education sector in the late twentieth century compounded this linguistic dominance. The irony is that the past decade has seen both these powers in the throes of a violent backlash against the globalization of which they were arguably the epicenters. Even as a vast portion of the world was learning to speak their language, the United States and the United Kingdom were throwing up further barriers to entry with travel bans, immigration restrictions, and increasingly elaborate citizenship requirements.

Perhaps the thirst for English is unsurprising. Learning English leads to higher education and job opportunities in the United States and the United Kingdom, as well as wage boosts of up to 15 percent in many other countries, including France, Austria, and Germany. No one needs a reporter to explain why people are learning English: the reasons are, as they say, self-evident.

My mother always emphasized the importance of mastering English in America. She had never managed to shed her 'Chinese accent,' having immigrated after her formative language development years. I was the mouth into which she fed her hopes of assimilation. We were always listening to public radio: American voices proclaimed the news to us over breakfast, and their confident banter crowded the car as my mother drove me to school.

I sometimes wonder if what first drew me to radio and print was the childhood dream of speaking on neutral ground. On the street, Asian tourists hailed me for directions, and Caucasian men leered 'Ni hao!' at me, though I did not speak Mandarin. But in your ear, or on the page, I was stripped of the face that rendered my voice foreign to other Americans. By the time I began working in public radio in my twenties, I had shed the tonal lilts of my first language, Cantonese, and cultivated a casual American cadence. Colleagues complimented my 'good radio voice' and 'neutral accent.'[5] On the radio, people no longer asked me 'where I was from.' I had become a voice that Americans could trust, the neutral voice critical to journalism: the reporting 'I,' the objective eye.

But there was still a problem, as I was told in my early interview training. You need to be more assertive, a senior colleague instructed me. You're too quiet; don't be afraid to interrupt the guest. If they don't give you the answer you want, take the mic back – he thrust the microphone away from

---

5 According to O.E.D., the American 'neutral accent,' also known as 'General American,' is a 'form of U.S. speech without marked dialectical or regional characteristics.' Wikipedia puts the case more bluntly: 'General American is perceived by most Americans to be "accent-less," meaning a person who speaks in such a manner does not appear to be from anywhere.' Ironically, the entry then states in great detail the regional minutia of where this accent can be located: 'The region of the United States that most resembles this is the central Midwest, specifically eastern Nebraska (including Omaha and Lincoln), southern and central Iowa (including Des Moines), parts of Missouri, Indiana, Ohio and western Illinois (including Peoria and the Quad cities, but not the Chicago area).' These areas are also sometimes referred to by politicians as the 'Real America,' locating the country's core identity with blue-collar whites in small Midwestern towns and rural locales. Incidentally, all the states listed, with the exception of Illinois, voted for Donald Trump in 2016, suggesting a distinctly partisan bent to these regions bearing 'neutral' accents.

me, and held it to his own lips – y'know, use your mic to control the conversation. It's like a power stick: whoever has the mic has the power to speak. Never let the guest take it from you. What I heard was: you must be loud and aggressive to succeed in America; to report on others, you must teach them how to speak.

What I heard was: you must be loud and aggressive to succeed in America; to report on others, you must teach them how to speak

But I did not want to wield the microphone like a foam-tipped phallus. I thought about telling him my mother's Chinese saying, 'Fang pey mo-cho, cho pey mo-fang': there is greater power in silence. (A more literal translation: 'Loud farts don't smell, silent farts are deadliest.') It struck me as a particularly apt critique of American public radio, in which many popular talk show hosts were loud gasbags who constantly talked over their own guests. I was as American as any of them, born and raised in the States. But by then, I was growing towards a different kind of speech, a way of giving voice to the unspoken. I was drawn to minorities and migrants, and to create margins wide enough for them – to create the space for *my* voice – required a great deal of silence.

I was not, in fact, 'quiet': I was listening.

I am always surprised by how many people forget that listening is also a speech act. Even the reporter who learns to efface herself with a 'neutral accent' presents a position: *everyone* comes from somewhere.

In reporting, an hour of tape is edited down to a 10-minute excerpt. A week-long conference is condensed into a 5000-word feature. Both are crafted to tell a story or raise a question: the ratio of silence and speech converge into meaning. When done well, the perception of natural conversation holds, the impression of neutrality persuades. In a certain accent, in an inviting tone, the interviewee hears a voice that says: trust me, I will listen to you. And it is true. As a reporter, I will give you the first word; I will give you the most words. I will always leave room for you. But ultimately, the last word will be mine – even when it is coming out of your mouth.

On the last day of the congress, I sat down to interview the President of Esperanto-USA. I had already heard about Orlando from the others; he was well-respected and liked, a middle-aged Cuban immigrant and chemistry professor with a jovial manner. His eyes creased with warmth when we shook hands, and he dimpled at me as he eased into the chair.

'I hope you've had a good time,' he said, as I flicked on my recorder and checked his sound levels. 'Have people been willing to open up?'

'Definitely,' I assured him. 'Everyone's been very generous with their time and stories.'

'Good, good.' He seemed pleased. 'I wasn't sure – you see, some Esperantists are quite shy. There have been reporters, in the past, who came to mock us. Look at these freaks, that kind of thing. But I've heard you are a good listener.'

'Glad to hear it.' I smiled. 'It's been an honor.'

'Ours, too.' His teeth gleamed against his walnut complexion. 'Have you found everything you're looking for?'

'Well, there's still something I am curious about,' I said. 'This special trust Esperantists keep talking about. I've heard many stories about Esperantists taking each other into their homes – complete strangers, from different countries. If Esperanto became truly global, if it became as widespread as English, would you still give your keys to strangers? If everyone spoke Esperanto?'

His brows lifted, and he chuckled. 'I don't think that's going to happen any time soon. Look, I know some Esperantists still believe in *la interna ideo*, this *fina venko* business, like Zamenhof.' He gave me a sly look. 'But that is not why I became an Esperantist,' he confessed. 'I've been an Esperantist for ages – since before I came to America, 25 years ago. I learned Esperanto when I was just a boy in Cuba, a little islander who wanted to explore the world. I believed it could open up the world for me, and it did. I've traveled so many places. Always, Esperantists opening their homes to me.'

For a moment, I envisioned this way of traveling the world, unfettered by ethnicity or national borders. Orlando's features were Cuban, and his English similarly inflected: I wondered if he received special treatment as the President of Esperanto-USA, or if he exaggerated to represent the community well. I returned to a suspicion that had been growing in me throughout the congress. 'Esperanto has a very noble vision of global harmony, and it seems like you manage to live it out among yourselves,' I said, choosing my words carefully. 'But you are a relatively small, tight-knit community – even though you are spread out across many countries. I wonder if this special bond you have in fact depends on its own kind of exclusivity: the fact that you are part of this special club. If exclusivity is in fact *essential* to creating that community.'

There was a time when my parents believed that if they could speak English properly ... the United States would embrace them as its own

I almost, but did not, say: like English. There was a time when my parents believed that if they could speak English properly, if they only worked hard enough, the United States would embrace them as its own. But as I moved through English-speaking countries with my American accent and Chinese face, I was increasingly made to realize that English – language itself – served as both a barrier and a bridge between peoples. That it could be weaponized in an instant. And I was growing exhausted by the constant effort of self-translation to people who would only listen to me on their own terms, and sometimes not even then.

Orlando must have read the despondence on my face, this man who had learned English late in life and spoke it with a thick, plosive accent. Because he smiled, and then said gently, 'Let us take off our masks for a moment. You as reporter, I as president.' He nodded at the blinking red eye of my recorder.

I considered, and then switched it off and put down my microphone. What followed next was not on record: a private fantasy.

There is some truth to what you suggest, he told me. If Esperanto became like English, maybe we would not have this big happy family. Maybe we would create our own borders, protect our little club.

He combed his fingers through his sparse hair, a tired crease at his eyes. Then he reconsidered: But on the other hand, Esperanto is *not* English. It is not, as you say, a natural language. There is no power or blood behind it – no country colonizes with it, few children inherit it. No one needs to learn it. It survives only because, in every generation since Zamenhof, a small number of people *choose* to learn it. Who believe, maybe, they can use it to connect with others, or create a kinder world. These are not the people who have determined history so far: they speak too softly, no one listens to them.

It is not ... a natural language. There is no power or blood behind it – no country colonizes with it ... no one needs to learn it

He paused. But who knows? Maybe, the day that everyone speaks Esperanto will be the day that everyone chooses to speak in a different kind of voice – one that lives by love, one that listens to others. We can only hope.

I asked: and do you believe in that day yourself?

His gaze darted to the blank eye of the recorder, and he sighed. No, I do not. I myself am a pragmatist. In real life, I am a scientist, a professor of chemistry. I do think Esperanto is rational, egalitarian – but people are not. I tell my students, if humankind was rational, everyone would adopt the metric system. But here we are, still measuring things in gallons, yards, feet.

We were silent for a moment, and then he shrugged. My goal as president has always been to keep the language alive for the community I love. I have little interest in evangelizing Esperanto, because – as I say – the world is neither rational nor fair.

Then why are you smiling? I asked.

I am smiling, he said, because I think *you* are in fact an Esperantist at heart, my objective reporter friend. His dark eyes crinkled at me. You are the one, not me, who keeps returning to *la interna ideo*.

I did have to fight to report on Esperanto, I said. But I must confess, I didn't even try to learn the language for the congress. And I probably won't ever.

It doesn't matter, he said. I told you, Esperanto is not like English; it is a language of the heart, and you can know it, belong to us, without speaking a word of it.

I laughed, startled. His eyes squinted with mirth. For several minutes, we were wordlessly bent over with bright, boisterous laughter. His audacity in embracing me as an Esperantist surprised me. But I forgave him for laying claim to me, because there was a warmth to his presumption, a kind of sweetness to his embrace – 'sweet' was indeed a good word for Esperanto. His declaration felt like the welcome inverse of my encounter with the bus driver, who had dismissed me from the community of English-speakers, despite my fluency with the language. Returning the president's words with a smile felt like a compromise I was willing to make.

He walked me out of the university building, and we said goodbye. I stood blinking in the summer heat for several moments. As I walked along the rustling elm walkway to the street, the noise of traffic began to reach my ears. In the distance, a yellow vintage convertible stopped at a traffic light. It blared a folk song whose melody was familiar, but whose name I had forgotten – something about a candle and many miles to Babylon. I paused to listen, trying to remember the words, but then the traffic light turned, and it whistled away. **H**

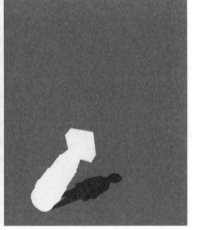

LITTLE BOY
by John Smith

ISBN 9781913861063

"Little Boy is an extraordinary novel, audacious and poignant and superbly well-written. It imagines the unimaginable, finds innocence in awfulness. This is what the literary novel is capable of, but so rarely pulls off..."

– Andrew Cowan

Editor's Choice, *The Bookseller*

BOILER HOUSE PRESS

Treasure

70 Hinterland

by Bonnie Lander Johnson

I n the British Library is a sixteenth-century manuscript written by an anonymous sailor. It describes Francis Drake's raid of a Spanish ship off the coast of El Salvador. Sent by Elizabeth I to take from land or sea whatever he could get in the way of gold, spices or drugs, Drake took everything on board the ship, including human cargo. The sailor's handwriting is difficult to decipher, knotted lines of browning ink stretch across the page unevenly. But steady transcription focuses an over-active mind so I work for two full hours in silence, until there's one line I cannot read beyond.

Now I stand on the South Bank beside Drake's own ship, the *Golden Hind*. It's a replica – about as real as the dubbing Drake is said to have received at the hands of a jubilant queen when she stepped on board the moment he reached English shores. Drake's knighthood was probably delivered instead by proxy and in the comfort of a hall. But history has held onto the image of the queen and her privateer exchanging grace for looted goods right there on the ship's deck.

Slaves unnumbered and unnamed travelled on the *Hind*, and some returned to England. But few can be traced in the archives. I still use paper and pencil in the library's rare books room. I also take pictures on my phone, like everyone else, but too many images crowding together in the photo file become meaningless. With a pencil I must be careful to transcribe correctly and be economical in what I take away. The piece of paper is in my pocket as I stand near the replica ship. On it is written the name of the slave woman that Drake took from the Spanish along with gold. Maria is what they called her, the name recorded by the sailor. A 'wench' who 'was afterward gotten with child between the captain and his men' before she was 'set on a small island to take her adventure.'

Perhaps we haven't asked the right questions. Why does my body kill half of my babies?

There was a baby in my belly until my body killed it. I'm standing on the deck of the *Golden Hind* bleeding heavily for the ninth week in a row. My disease isn't rare at all but we know very little about it. Perhaps we haven't asked the right questions. Why does my body kill half of my babies? Why did Drake leave a pregnant woman on an island? What other sixteenth-century uses of 'adventure' does the OED definition contain? To dare, to undertake, to venture, as in Shakespeare's *Pericles*: 'To taste the fruit of yon celestial tree, / Or die in the adventure.' That's the sort of journey we all dream about. But Maria's life was put to adventure – as in to imperil, to expose to danger, as in More's *Richard III*: 'For what wise merchant adventureth all his good in one ship.'

That evening I take the children to *A Midsummer Night's Dream* in the botanic gardens: fairy lights, fireflies, rugs and pillows piled high on the dew-dappled grass. They laugh with the clowns and wonder at Oberon's magic but they will not notice or remember the description of the unnamed pregnant woman, her round belly compared by Titania to a merchant ship heavy with gold and spices.

The child is her delight. She crowns him with flowers, she covers him with kisses

Unlike Elizabeth I, Titania has wings and can travel the globe in an arc as wide as the circle Drake drew through the world's blue water. On her voyage, Titania has acquired a beautiful Indian boy. The child is her delight. She crowns him with flowers, she covers him with kisses. She refuses to share him with her jealous husband because, she says, his mother was a devotee, a votress of Titania's order, a worshipper at the altar of the Fairy Queen. To Titania the boy's mother brought trifles as they sat together on the Bay of Bengal, breathing the spiced air and gossiping as pregnant women do when they are too big to do much else. Titania will not give that boy away, she says, because his mother made her promise to raise him up should the perilous adventure of childbirth take her to that most distant shore.

Can a child be given away? Oberon has a different story to tell, one in which Titania stole the baby from an Indian King. It's the kind of thing fairies used to do: swap babies, take away sick babies or those whose mothers were too poor to feed them. But Oberon says that this child is well, more than well, and loved, loved by royalty – the boy is a prince, no mere trifle for a fairy to crown with flowers and carry about like a bauble plucked from a merchant at sea. But when he retrieves the boy from Titania, what does Oberon do with him? I wrap up my children in blankets. They fell asleep during the final act. As we ride home the stars flash across the sky almost as bright as they must be when seen above the ocean with your back pressed against the deck of a ship.

The list of items Elizabeth I wanted Drake to bring to her goes like this: gold, silver, spices, drugs, cochineal, and 'divers other special commodities such as may enrich her highness' dominions.' You wouldn't think that the item of the greatest personal value to Elizabeth I was the cochineal. It's a small red bug – thought at the time to be a berry or flower. But used as a dye it produces a red colour more deep and rich and noble than any of the dyes Elizabeth I could get her hands on at home. Cochineal was guarded by the Spanish with military strength; it was what we would now call a state secret. No one but a small group of Spanish noblemen knew the location of their King's cochineal production, concentrated in one small area of Mexico.

For all his gold and spices, Drake's greatest political achievement was the looting of twenty-seven tonnes of cochineal from a Spanish ship. So much red! In Elizabethan sumptuary laws, no person could wear red except the monarch and their family. But Elizabeth I had no family. The shipload of cochineal was a gift out of all proportion: the greatest riches of the world, unlocked from the most secretive source, for one woman alone.

You might wonder if Elizabeth I's desire for red concealed some subtext and you wouldn't be the first to do so. Whispers about her body's ability to make life out of blood followed her through the sixteenth century. At around the time her period ought to have started, the girl with the golden hair embroidered a book cover. A gift to her stepmother. The contents of the book was Elizabeth I's own translation of a philosophical work by a French queen connected to the long line of Tudor women scholars. On the cover of the book she embroidered her stepmother's initials and four red pansies – a pun on the French pensée, 'thought,' and a mark of the very red Tudor blood running through her own young body. It's a sad sign of how subtle children can be when they try to secure love. But the cloth that wove the pansies was dyed with safflowers, not with cochineal. It soon faded to the kind of brown that blood becomes when it's spilled and spoiled.

Pansies, violets, primroses. Small flowers that grow wild in the garden in early spring. The children pluck the petals and mix them with water in a bowl and leave it as an offering to the fairy who lives in the oversized apple tree that grows too close to the house. Pansies were Elizabeth I's signature flower. The rose belonged to the Tudor line but she alone was the 'pretty pansy,' her gloves perfumed with that flower's odour and her dresses embroidered with its small petalled faces.

Last year an altar cloth was discovered in a village church on the edge of London. It had been lying in plain sight but someone decided it was in fact Elizabeth I's undergarment. Covered in pansies sewn with thread still now as red as living blood. Cochineal, the blood that never dies. Those secretive Spanish noblemen had workers in Mexico whose hands were perpetually red with cochineal. Locals and human cargo brought from the Ivory Coast. When Maria had her baby on that lonely island, was it born into hands as red as the flowers that grew so like to life on Elizabeth I's undergarment, now spread on the altar of a church that stands alone in its green fields? That baby had a baby who had a baby.

Covered in pansies sewn with thread still now as red as living blood. Cochineal, the blood that never dies

To steal back the baby Titania stole from the Indian throne, Oberon tells Puck to circumnavigate the world. A bright fairy line spun from the Forest of Arden in a girdle all around the Earth's wide belly. From this journey Puck must bring that precious magic flower, the pansy known as love-

in-idleness. With its juice Oberon will induce in
his wife a sexual desire so potent and beastly that
Titania will cease to think of her Indian boy.
Oberon tells a story about that flower, a white pansy
stained with the dark vermeil of love's wound.
He says the flower was pure white until Elizabeth I
passed by 'in maiden meditation, fancy free.'
In the sky above, Cupid spied the queen and shot
his love shaft toward her. But she, being chaste,
walked undisturbed. Instead the arrow landed in
the little white pansy, which to this day is bruised
with stripes of unwanted love.

Drake had two wives, Mary who died and then Elizabeth who watched him die

Drake had two wives, Mary who died and then
Elizabeth who watched him die. Neither woman
bore a child – his babies are all at sea. I try and
see inside the man's heart but last month we took
the children back to Ireland where blood once
ran in the streets and onto the shores of Rathlin.
There's nothing so beautiful as the view across
the bay from Rathlin when the sun pours emerald
over the grass-topped cliff that descends to the
water in a sweep of grey and silver scree. The
white shoreline slips into deep blue waters and the
lonely ruin of the old chapel stands brazen against
the tide. From inside the cave you can see the sea
through the tall line of the cave-mouth's ragged
stone edge, as it would have been when Elizabeth I
knew it, except she never knew it with her own face.

The rebel clanswomen hid themselves and their children inside that cave but they did not hide for long. Island caves were Drake's currency, the sea his moving stage. Blood runs like a carpet from the cave-mouth and is washed away.

I try to see inside the heart of him. There is in all men a desperate hunger for love and in all women too. The British Library holds a manuscript that illustrates a female anatomy of the kind Elizabeth I would have known. Not personally – she would not have the integrity of her body undermined even by leeches. Nor did she ever wield a sword. Her cuts were ordered with the pen. What a pen! I am told the only thing for me is to have it all cut out, that troublesome bag of blood. But my disease is not so rare. I walk the children to school and count the mothers at the gate and wonder how many carry empty caves inside them.

In Oxburgh Hall hang carpets embroidered by Mary Queen of Scots. She was one for the plants and flowers: fat fish and blousy roses, bare trees and tigers. Not a pansy or primrose to be found. They say it took four strokes of the axe to get her head off and her mouth kept praying long after the last nerve severed. I thought those executioners were experts. Oxburgh has a cave in the floor under a wardrobe where they hid priests from the same axe. I go down inside it to say my prayer but the mouth is so narrow I almost can't get out.

Long before Oberon's love potion came into being, Shakespeare's mind was already turning on Elizabeth I's pansy. The theatres closed against the plague, Shakespeare travelled home to write in couplets his Venus who so desired the young Adonis that she abased herself. She lay at his feet, begged to be kissed by him, her heart a desert with wanting of that cruel boy. But Adonis preferred hunting and in the end the boar stuck him so deep the blood ran from his thigh into the dirt where Venus knelt weeping. Then from Adonis' blood sprung up a flower, vermeil and white. She plucked it from its stem and slipped it between her breasts. 'Poor flower,' she said. 'In this hollow cradle take they rest … sweet issue of a more sweet-smelling sire.' She rocked the dying flower day and night beside her 'throbbing heart' and promised that 'there shall not be one minute in an hour, wherein I will not kiss my sweet love's flower.'

The bag bobs swollen to the surface, blood pouring from it in a bright red stream

In the British Library is a book of dye recipes of the kind Elizabeth I would have known. Take one pound of red flowers and soak them in milk for one day and one night, then put them in a cloth bag and rinse them in the river until the bag is red. Wring out the bag and dry the flowers, then grind them with white ash and vinegar. I take the children to the edge of the Thames with a pillowcase full of flowers. We push the bag into the shallow water where Coke cans and bike wheels snag against the silted floor. The bag bobs swollen to the surface, blood pouring from it in a bright red stream. That

night I dream a terrible dream. A ship loaded with
cochineal, gold and the bruised bodies of slaves is
sucked into the muddy water of the Thames until
barely an inch of its topmast can be seen above
the bubbling surface of the river. From within the
belly of the ship, the cochineal unfurls and floats
away until all the water from Limehouse to London
Bridge is drenched in blood of a red so bright that it
will never fade. ∎

Throwing the

Dice Again

by *Tom Bailey*

I

If Charles Causley is known for anything, it's probably for the fact that he's being forgotten. Hardly anyone writes about him, and among the few critics who do, a phrasebook has emerged, a lexicon of shared sentiment. *Neglected, undervalued, overlooked*: words like these are never far from a mention of his work. Ironically, this risks becoming his only claim to fame – the poet lost to history.

But commonplaces are commonplace for a reason. Even among poetry lovers, the name Charles Causley is increasingly unfamiliar. Most people have never heard of him at all.

—

But this hasn't always been the case. Causley was once routinely cited among the UK's best living poets. He was given a Queen's Gold Medal for Poetry in 1967 and awarded a CBE in 1986. He was a favourite for the laureateship – before being offered the job himself, Hughes had said the role should go to Causley. Alongside Heaney, Hughes, and Larkin, Causley was one of the four judges for the 1980 Arvon Poetry Prize. Heaney, Larkin, Hughes: three names we hear often. But not Causley.

Towards the end of his long life, Causley's reputation began to fade. By 1997, one critic had labelled him 'the most unfashionable poet alive.'

—

In Alan Bennett's annual diary from 2003, published January 2004, there's this entry for Wednesday, June 11th –

> Why isn't more fuss made over Charles Causley? Looking through his *Collected Poems* to copy out his 'Ten Types of Hospital Visitor' I dip into some of his other poems, so many of them vivid and memorable. Well into his eighties, he must be one of the most distinguished poets writing today (if he still is). But why does nobody say so and celebrate him while he's still around? Hurrah for Charles Causley is what I say. [Too late. He dies 4 November.]

Hurrah, nonetheless.

—

So why has Causley fallen out of favour? It's hard to say. He wrote ballads and children's poems – perhaps unfashionable forms in a post-confessional era. Open up his voice, and you'll find Hardy and Auden inside. Lorca is also hanging around somewhere, decked out in bow tie and jacket.

But Causley was more than a ballad poet: most of his best poems are short lyrics. Detractors call him conservative, but it's hardly a fitting description. For all his use of traditional forms, his work is always deeply original. Causley may be accessible, but the way he uses language is unsettling and new. His words splash us awake. His poems are peopled by strangeness: men with 'accents like tin-openers', trees 'screaming with starlings', and children who wear 'insults like flowers'. Dickinson is here, surely, in the surrealism of these similes. The sun comes like a killer out of the park. A heart falls like a bucket down a well.

Causley may be accessible, but the way he uses language is unsettling and new. His words splash us awake

II

But let me begin again. If there's one thing that Charles Causley *should* be known for, it's his endings: the final lines of his poems. Anyone who knows Causley will know what I'm talking about. They will likely have a final line in mind, a personal favourite. Maybe the sonically playful ending of Causley's 'Magpie': 'He struts in the dust. Bullies a whiskey jack.' Or the final line of 'The Prodigal Son', with its mystical ambiguity: 'Out of the sun's dazzle, somebody spoke my name.' Or maybe the end of 'King's College Chapel': 'They sit in their white lawn sleeves, as cool as history.'

This is hardly a revelatory claim, but final lines tend to be pretty important. If you ask me, they're often the most important line of a poem – the final words we hear before the voice falls silent.

The end of a poem is the poem's edge, a point of definition. Some edges are sharper than others, of course, but they are edges nevertheless. If only by its position at the end of a poem, an 'ending' carries the burden of meaning-making – even if it shies away from any clear meaningfulness.

—

The first Causley I ever read was his lyric 'Eden Rock', probably his most famous poem:

Eden Rock
They are waiting for me somewhere beyond Eden Rock:
My father, twenty-five, in the same suit
Of Genuine Irish Tweed, his terrier Jack
Still two years old and trembling at his feet.

My mother, twenty-three, in a sprigged dress
Drawn at the waist, ribbon in her straw hat,
Has spread the stiff white cloth over the grass.
Her hair, the colour of wheat, takes on the light.

She pours tea from a Thermos, the milk straight
From an old H.P. sauce-bottle, a screw
Of paper for a cork; slowly sets out
The same three plates, the tin cups painted blue.

The sky whitens as if lit by three suns.
My mother shades her eyes and looks my way
Over the drifted stream. My father spins
A stone along the water. Leisurely,

They beckon to me from the other bank.
I hear them call, 'See where the stream-path is!
Crossing is not as hard as you might think.'

I had not thought that it would be like this.

I had not thought that it would be like this. In a documentary about Causley's life, the poet Andrew Motion said that if he could write a line as perfect as this, he would die a happy man.

—

I had not thought that it would be like this. It takes me by surprise every time, the way the poem seems to step back from itself, giving us this single sentence of authorial commentary. It's like Causley has painted this scene for us – the picnic on the opposite bank, his mother and father calling him across. And then, putting down his palette, he looks for the first time at the canvas.

'Eden Rock' is the final poem in ... the very last book he published, making this final line the last of all his published work

Which gives the pleasing suggestion that the 'it' of the poem's final line may in fact refer not only to the afterlife, but perhaps to the poem itself: I had not thought that the poem would be like this. Or even that the final line may refer to its own unexpectedness – I had not thought that the poem would *end* like this.

But it's worth noting that this line is an ending in more ways than one. 'Eden Rock' is the final poem in Causley's Collected Poems, the very last book he published, making this final line the last of all his published work. It's a fitting finale: a poem about the end of his own life.

—

I had not thought that it would be like this. I can't help but be reminded of the end of Ted Hughes's 'Hawk Roosting', with its instantly unforgettable final line: 'I am going to keep things like this.'

The two poems both end with the same two words, and both involve a similar 'stepping back'. But there's nothing of Hughes's braggishness in Causley's final line. For a start, the Hughes poem is expressing a determination for the future, whereas Causley's 'Eden Rock' ends with a confession of previous ignorance. And the Causley ending is more subtle in its tone: despite its monosyllabic beat, there's something fragile and tentative about its rocking movement.

Where, after all, do our stresses go? There are no nouns to carry the syllabic weight of the sentence, no word on which we can hang our emphasis. It's difficult to read. It feels like tetrameter with a clumsy pair of words snagged on the end, *like this*. Read it aloud and your voice fades slightly after be, and the poem seems to close with a dying fall.

III

Marianne Moore is another poet whose endings are worthy of fame. Her poems close like magic tricks. With a flourish of her black cape, she leaves us standing awkwardly around, wondering how we got there, and what on earth happened.

Take her poem 'Silence', for example, which begins quite benignly: 'My father used to say…' But

the end of the poem can't help but leave us winded.
It's simple, yes, but also strangely threatening:

> Nor was he insincere in saying, "Make my
>   house your inn."
> Inns are not residences.

The poem is 14 lines long, so I guess these
bewildering closing lines are Moore's take on a
Shakespearean couplet. The first twelve lines are in
her father's voice, with Moore apparently absent.
But now, in these final words, at the very edge of
the poem, we hear her own voice for the first time:
Inns are not residences.

Marianne Moore's *Complete Poems* was prefaced
with the words: 'Omissions are not accidents.' I
don't imagine this echo was an accident, either.

———

I had not thought that it would be like this. Until we
reach this final line, everything is present-tense
description, the poem gathering details as it moves:
the terrier Jack, the Thermos, the H.P. Sauce bottle.
Description, here, is an act of filial love. Look at his
father's Irish Tweed, his mother's 'sprigged dress /
Drawn at the waist'. Objects build up. Everything
feels so delicate, so carefully in its place: the stiff
white picnic cloth, the plates set out with 'the tin
cups painted blue.' But there's a quiet sense of
fragility too, as if the dream might suddenly end.
As if everything might abruptly fall apart.

Marianne Moore's 'No Swan So Fine' is the sort of poem that ought to have a 'Handle With Care' sticker. In two densely spondaic stanzas, the poem describes a swan made of 'chintz china' with 'fawn- / brown eyes and toothed gold / collar'. This is Moore at her best, pushing language to its limits, her words sculpting a candelabrum of sound, of cockscomb-tinted buttons and sea urchins. The poem is like a game of Jenga: every time a word is added on top, the tower wobbles and threatens to tumble down. And this is how it ends:

> it perches on the branching foam
> of polished sculptured
> flowers – at ease and tall. The king is dead.

Those final four words come utterly out of nowhere: *The King is dead*. And the poem is pulled out from underneath us.

Those final four words come utterly out of nowhere: *The King is dead*. And the poem is pulled out from underneath us

IV

Some final lines are like doors swung shut. You know the ones, like James Wright's 'Lying in a Hammock at William Duffy's Farm in Pine Island, Minnesota'.

In many ways it's very simple: the poet is lying in a hammock, describing what he sees. It's a poem of images, where one description is followed by another and another. First a bronze butterfly, then the sound of cowbells, then a field of sunlight between two pine trees. Then something else happens:

> I lean back, as the evening darkens and
>   comes on.
> A chicken hawk floats over, looking for home.
> I have wasted my life.

The ending changes everything, like a needle popping a balloon.

—

The thing about a poem is that it does have to end at some point. It's the unspoken agreement between a poet and their reader: no matter how long the poem is, thankfully it won't go on forever. Readers will not be held hostage, like the dinner-guests in Buñuel's *Exterminating Angel* who find themselves unable to leave the table.

'There is a distinction, however,' Barbara Herrnstein Smith argues in her book *Poetic Closure*, 'between concluding and merely stopping or ceasing. The ringing of a telephone, the blowing of the wind, the babbling of an infant in its crib: these stop. A poem or a piece of music concludes.'

Smith is a scholar of Shakespeare's sonnets, which is no surprise really: the sonnets are poems that end with conviction, often with concise and gnomic lines. Take the final couplet of 'Sonnet 30':

> But if the while I think on thee, dear friend,
> All losses are restor'd, and sorrows end.

To end a poem on the word 'end' – it's like a box closing with a satisfying click, or maybe a hymn book slapped shut at the end of a church service. That's what the heavy rhyme is saying: the poem is over and done with. Scurry on home through the snow.

—

I have wasted my life. Only when I taught Wright's poem did I realize quite how funny it is. Funny, but also somehow devastating. I won't try to open up and unpack that final line, but I will mention another important end that Wright echoes, Rainer Maria Rilke's 'Archaic Torso of Apollo', which describes the poet's encounter with a sculpture. And as with the Wright poem, Rilke's ending seems to come out of nowhere. After several lines of ekphrastic description, we are left with a simple five-word sentence: *You must change your life.*

To end a poem on the word 'end' – it's like a box closing with a satisfying click, or maybe a hymn book slapped shut at the end of a church service

> Some final lines are like doors swung shut, but others swing open like windows. That's the difference between Rilke's line and Wright's. Both

endings are unexpected, but they couldn't be more different. Wright's looks back, but Rilke's looks forward. Imperatives, after all, are acts of expectation, not of closure. Wright pops a party balloon; Rilke gives you one of your own to fill up with air.

—

Speaking of balloons: Sylvia Plath's 'Morning Song' – a poem describing the first night with a new-born at home. Dawn comes at the end of the poem, which closes with an image not of closure but of change:

> The window square
>
> Whitens and swallows its dull stars. And now you try
> Your handful of notes;
> The clear vowels rise like balloons.

This is what Smith might call 'weak closure', a style of ending she sees as characteristic of 'modern' writing. These poems refuse to close with a click of the latch. But 'weak' is not a value judgement. In many cases, weak closure is the most successful kind. For Smith, these open-ended endings convey doubt and tentativeness, a refusal 'to make absolute and unqualified assertions.' Plath leaves us with a powerful image, but a delicate one at that: hope, here, is a fragile thing.

V

It's hard to end a poem. It's hard to do so without
a strained 'here's-what-I-want-you-to-understand'
effect. The best poems are attentive to this
difficulty, and they play with our expectations of
what a final line should be. They walk the tightrope
between closure and anti-closure, between ending
and not-ending.

Or maybe they end by refusing to end: a blurring
at the edge. Like Heaney's poem 'Personal Helicon',
with its beautiful final stanza:

> Now, to pry into roots, to finger slime,
> To stare, big-eyed Narcissus, into some spring
> Is beneath all adult dignity. I rhyme
> To see myself, to set the darkness echoing.

The poem ends quite emphatically, with an
aphoristic final phrase, a turn from past to present,
and even a quiet rhyme in the words 'spring' and
'echoing'. But 'echoing' is a suggestive word with
which to end a poem. What is an echo, in any
case, but a refusal of sound to end? In other words,
Heaney's voice is still echoing down the well, and
the poem continues even after its final line.

———

There's a tension here between endings and not-
endings, between closure and its lack, and we
see the same thing in Causley's sequence 'Scenes

from Childhood'. The final poem, 'Forbidden Games', remembers playing *Snakes & Ladders* the day his father died. Here are the poem's last lines, beginning with the quoted speech of either his aunt or mother:

> 'Your father's with the angels now.'
> Which of them speaks I cannot tell.
> And then I say to them, 'I know.'
> And give the dice another throw.

VI

I've been thinking about that final line again: *I had not thought that it would be like this.* So much signals the end of the poem: the shift in tense, the stepping-back, the iambic pentameter. But still the line refuses any heavy-handed finality. It's far too ambiguous for that, too aware of itself as a final line.

It certainly isn't a resolution in any straightforward sense: there are still several loose threads that the poem leaves us with. We're told that the speaker had not thought that 'it' would be like this, but we're not told what he actually thought it *would* be like. His parents beckon him across the river, but we aren't given any indication of whether he makes it across. *Crossing is not as hard as you might think*, perhaps, but it could still be very hard.

—

I had not thought that it would be like this. Perhaps the most obvious literary allusion is, via Eliot, to Dante's *Inferno*: 'I had not thought death had undone so many.'

I had not thought is itself an odd and slightly clunky phrase, so this allusion could very well be conscious. After all, both Causley and Dante are writing about afterlives. But Dante's line comes very early on in *The Divine Comedy – Inferno III*, the scene at the gates of Hell. This is really the beginning of Dante's journey. So if Causley's final line is an intentional echo of Dante, it does suggest that this ending is not really an ending at all, but a beginning.

Which is why the poem's title is so relevant. Causley was 83 years-old when 'Eden Rock' was published, but his parents here are young again, young as they were when Causley was a boy. Death leads the poet back to the early years of his life, where he becomes a small child once more on a picnic with his parents. The afterlife returns him to a pre-Lapsarian innocence, a literal genesis. Put simply: *In my end is my beginning.*

—

Causley once said: 'Somebody asked me the other day where Eden Rock is. I mean I have no idea – I made it up. Dartmoor, I said. That's always a safe answer.'

—

Endings are rarely final in Causley's work. Even death – that final ending – is not an actual end. I like to think of Causley as a poet of resurrections: 'Eden Rock' isn't the only poem where we find the dead alive. In 'By St Thomas Water', the bodies buried in the graveyard are 'not dead but sleeping', and in 'Death of a Poet', Causley's elegy for Louis MacNeice, the dead poet may not even be dead at all: 'I got the feeling you were curled up inside the box, listening.'

> **Endings are rarely final in Causley's work. Even death – that final ending – is not an actual end. I like to think of Causley as a poet of resurrections**

I should also mention Causley's poem 'Richard Bartlett', an elegy for his grandfather, a stone-cutter and quarryman. Bartlett was killed by a falling piece of slate, and his death is described to us in all of its violent detail:

> Nine on a July morning: Richard Bartlett
> About to split a stone, trying to find
> A place to insert the wedge. The overhang
> Shrugs off a quiet sting of slate. It nags
> Three inches through the skull. Richard Bartlett
> Never spoke after he was struck.

Bartlett never spoke again, but Causley speaks instead. In fact, the poem ends with Bartlett resurrected in the poet: in the poem's last line, we see Causley himself 'Bend to the poem, / Trying to find a place to insert the wedge.' With that direct repetition,

Charles Causley becomes Richard Bartlett, bending over a stone; and Richard Bartlett becomes Charles Causley, bending over the poem. Where Heaney in 'Digging' digs like his father, Causley's pen is cutting stone like Richard Bartlett did.

Some endings rise like balloons. Some echo beyond themselves. And others throw the dice all over again

So death is not really an ending, because the dead live on in the living. And the ending, here, takes us back to the poem's origin, when Causley the poet sat down and began to write it, 'Trying to find a place to insert the wedge.' It's a sort of recursive loop wherein the poem begins again and again every time it ends. Which is to say, *In my end is my beginning*.

VII

One of the problems with how we talk about endings – specifically poetic endings – is that we often think of them as destinations. The poem is pictured as a train travelling from one place to another, and then it comes to a halt in a railway station: readers disembark with their luggage. Certainly some poems work like that, but there are plenty more that don't. Some endings rise like balloons. Some echo beyond themselves. And others throw the dice all over again.

—

For all my attachment to his poems, I must also admit an attachment to the man. Causley is an underdog, and that's probably why I like him. He's compared by some to Hughes and Larkin but he isn't of their ilk. Hughes and Larkin went to Oxbridge, but Causley left school at fifteen. Apart from his time in the navy, he lived his life in the village where he was born: Launceston, Cornwall. He became a teacher at the national school where he had been a pupil. You can understand why Hughes called him 'a man of the people, in the old, best sense.'

But Causley is being forgotten. I admit this is probably also one of the reasons that I like him. There's something romantic about a poet whose work is barely known outside of Cornwall. He is like a private interest. I do not have to share him.

—

I had not thought that it would be like this. It's always struck me as incredibly sad, this line, though I don't know why exactly.

There's a recording of Causley reciting the poem on the online Poetry Archive. When he reaches the final three words, I almost think you can hear his voice shake . **H**

Charles Causley, 'Eden Rock' in *Collected Poems 1951-2000* London: Macmillan (2000), p. 421

Maintaining An

Ambivalent Art: Caring

by Constance Kresge

I do a hell of a lot of washing, cleaning, cooking,
renewing, supporting, preserving, etc. Also,
(up to now) separately I 'do' Art.

– Mierle Laderman Ukeles,
Manifesto for Maintenance Art 1969!
Proposal for an exhibition: 'CARE', 1969

I had written approximately seventeen words when I interrupted the writing of this essay for the first time to care for my daughter Josephine. It took two days for me to return. In this gap, I finished two loads of laundry, purchased groceries, cleaned the floors, swept up a broken bowl, unloaded and reloaded the dishwasher, changed multiple diapers, ordered Halloween costumes, cooked two dinners. There is no 'and' in that last sentence; its inclusion would imply a finality to the list. The list, in fact, lies more on the side of infinite.

Mierle Laderman Ukeles's *Manifesto for Maintenance Art* and her subsequent installations make no distinction between one's habitual or daily tasks and (A)rt. Her revelation came after the birth of her child, when she realized that the everyday tasks required to keep another person alive prevented her from 'doing' her Art. Therefore, she radically (or naturally? necessarily?) transformed the 'doing' into the Art. Laundry would become Art. Changing diapers and making oatmeal would become Art. She defines this concept – *Maintenance Art* – broadly and universally to include the sanitation workers who maintain our cities and even the Earth itself as it continually cleanses the water and air. What was habitual and ignored becomes ritualistic and reverential.

It is now the start of 2021, more than fifty years since Ukeles's *Manifesto,* which I read on my phone while ignoring my daughter. It occurs to me: America has come to revile and revere Maintenance. We no longer like to keep the streets swept or the bridges new. We purchase disposable razors and throw out dull knives and socks with holes in them. The nation's infrastructure is crumbling. 'Good jobs' innovate, disrupt, and redefine rather than require the same set of daily actions. An entire generation of youth was taken in by Silicon Valley and its promise that an app could do the work of civil society or government. I say we. Do I mean, rather, the blue-leaning, college-educated, grass-is-always-greener types who are willing to uproot themselves to join a startup in Austin or Portland or

Brooklyn, but not stay in Cleveland or Jacksonville to do the maintenance work (Art?) of petitioning for a community garden or attending their local city council meetings? (Guilty as charged.) The small work seems to have fallen out of fashion. And what requires more small work than parenting? To assist my transition to motherhood I relied upon the modern-day experts: Pinterest, Instagram, and the derisively termed 'mommy blogs', where I discovered that previously private and domestic tasks are now commoditized, packaged, and sold to help the time-crunched attend to the Art of Maintaining. Nearly every aspect of domestic life can be outsourced, improved or purchased readymade. A short list of domestic readymades for sale: toddler activity schedule | a month of slow cooker recipes | cleaning hacks | infant sleep schedules | holiday decorating kits. Perhaps we revere the small work when it can be sold.

Nearly every aspect of domestic life can be outsourced, improved or purchased readymade.

Decades before Ukeles created Art out of the everyday, and late-stage capitalism commodified it, Marcel Duchamp took common store-bought or found objects, ascribed his name to them, and held them up as Art. This is the description accompanying Duchamp's *In Advance of the Broken Arm* on the Museum of Modern Art's website:

These sculptures, which he called 'readymades',
were aimed at subverting traditional notions of
skill, uniqueness, and beauty, boldly declaring that
an artist could create simply by making choices.
Duchamp purchased the first version of this work in a
hardware store in 1915, signed and dated the shovel,
and hung it on display from his studio ceiling.

Duchamp bought a shovel, signed it, hung it up,
and called it Art. Ukeles wiped her child's bottom
and called it Art. Capitalism has taken something
potentially reverential – the care of one's child –
and commoditized it. I can call my deciding-what-
to-make-for-dinner Art, but it is also someone else's
job with venture-capital-backed funding, and it is
something I can purchase as a readymade via a
subscription service. If I enjoy Duchamp's shovel as
Art, can microwaving a meal or ordering takeout
count as Maintenance Art, or is there a level of
sacrifice required that cannot be substituted by a
readymade Maintenance? How much attention is
required to elevate this all to Art? If all that I do
for the sake of Care is Art, then much of my art is
admittedly Bad Art, performed with little attention,
with reluctance and even disdain – emotions I do
not sense from either Ukeles or Duchamp. How can
one keep up a perfect craft of this Art?

My youngest brother, Michael, is intellectually
disabled. Born when I was nearly six, he has a
profound mental disability that has kept him, in
some respects, at the age of a toddler. Today, aged
thirty-six, he requires someone else to change his

diapers and cook his food. He can put dishes in the dishwasher and make his bed but cannot consistently empty the dishwasher or successfully change his sheets. I have watched my mother *care* for my brother for nearly four decades. I have assisted my mother in *caring* for my brother. He is now in a group home where he is *cared* for by strangers.

The presence of Michael in my life has impacted me in untold ways. I have understood for a long time what it is like to have a young child. Even before the arrival of my daughter, I knew the generalities: how many minutes of each day would be spent picking up toys, how little privacy I would have in the bathroom, how little time could be spent in intellectual contemplation as 'Old MacDonald' played over and over again in the background. Right now, my daughter, at nineteen months, has learned the joy of throwing things in the trash. We've found stuffed animals, cups, and the dog's collar atop the remains of last night's dinner. My in-laws, despite having had two children of their own, find this amusing and novel. My brother lived through this stage for years. For me, the only novel part is that my daughter will grow out of this behavior rapidly. My brother did eventually mature in many ways, but the change could be painfully gradual. Thankfully he has moved past children's songs to more mature tastes such as Johnny Cash. Last night I spoke with one of Michael's caretakers, Jose, who informed me that his latest song on repeat is 'Apple Bottom Jeans', screaming *boots with the fur* at the top of his lungs.

People who have witnessed me around children have remarked on my Zen-like ability to simultaneously attend to a child's needs, remain unflustered, and continue an adult conversation. Many new parents struggle with this. They look away, forget what is being said, and constantly apologize for their children's actions. I (and yes, I'm proud of this) can flow like a mother of five. The child can wait while I converse, and block towers can be built while I maintain eye contact with a friend. But these are not skills I wanted to perfect in my twenties or early thirties. My own sanity and growth required that I not tend to, care for, think about, or worry for anyone else. This was clearly impossible, but I tried. I sought adventure and moved a lot: Germany, Mexico, Nicaragua, New York City, Chicago. But in between months of doing shots in Berlin nightclubs or backpacking through the Alaskan wilderness I continued to help with my brother; I just let myself have a bit of freedom. And the easiest way of doing this was to delay having children.

My own sanity and growth required that I not tend to, care for, think about, or worry for anyone else.

Before my brother found a place in his current group home, my family fretted about his long-term situation. None of us wanted the burden of caring for him full time. How could one maintain both a career and a family of one's own and take care of him around the clock? I grew up in Richmond, Virginia, where for a number of years, Michael attended a school for the intellectually disabled. He was a cheerleader for the basketball team and performed in school plays. He learned to use the restroom on his own. He flourished. Then the state cut funding and changed its policies. He was no longer eligible for the specialized school and was transferred to a local public school. He soon lost the ability to use the restroom himself, and we put him on a ten-year waitlist for permanent housing.

—

Here I stopped the essay again. It was weeks before the 2020 presidential election. An election that many, including me, felt could determine the future of our democracy. I could not justify spending my free hours musing over my feelings about taking

> **He soon lost the ability to use the restroom himself, and we put him on a ten-year waitlist for permanent housing.**

care of my daughter, especially when this election (and sadly every election) might determine the future of my brother's care. His current situation is supported by a patchwork of Easter Seals, Medicare, Medicaid, and state, local, and federal policies – all of which constantly feel at risk, and especially under a president who has publicly mocked those with disabilities. So for three weeks I contacted potential voters in Arizona, listening to voicemails and requests to stop calling. This volunteering was also Art, according to Ukeles, who in her *Manifesto* writes: '...after the revolution, who's going to pick up the garbage on Monday morning?' So, in addition to doing dishes and wiping a bottom as Art, I added phone banking to my portfolio. Even artists take breaks though, no?

My family ended up lucky. In 2006, my mother visited her sister in rural New Mexico. Tucked into the southern tip of the Rocky Mountains, with near-daily blue skies, northern New Mexico offered her not just a new lifestyle but also a sustainable one – there was no waitlist for my brother's care. She moved them there mere weeks after learning this, and within a year and a half my brother moved into a group home. It wasn't until he was securely cared for that I began to see my life options differently. I could, just maybe, forgo the law or finance path I had been on and quit scrimping every way I could – skipping meals, living with a roommate in a cheap apartment, saving every penny to help pay for someone other than my mother to care for Michael.

At the time I thought I was making self-directed choices. I see now how much the socio-economic and political system corralled me. The economics of care are often neglected. I recently stumbled upon a European corner of the internet exploring what the future of economics might look like via science-fiction thought experiments. It's a quirky, male-technocrat part of the world with in-depth musings on pricing theory, reputational credits, peer production, and abundance. But no work on their long list of science fiction deals with the care economy, except perhaps Ursula K. LeGuin's *The*

Dispossessed, and it only slightly. I see no attempt to answer the basic questions of who is caring for whom and how. When the population ages, will we continue to rely upon the cheapest labor available; be that migrants, disadvantaged minority groups, or artificial intelligence? Or will we build a more communitarian option? How does that square with envisioned notions of liberty and freedom?

Ukeles asks these questions. She gets it.

> *What is the relationship between maintenance and freedom?*
> *What is the relationship between maintenance and life's dreams?*

—

It is now months after I began this essay. Josephine is refusing her nap in the room next to me, and I am pushing through this sentence while she wails. At some point, my decision to have a child turned to a biological need. It felt like an electric current, or a magnetic field – something I imagine guiding the flight paths of migrating birds. Around age thirty-four this need became a requirement. I saw the funny pregnancy T-shirts, noted the locations of daycares, and imagined carrying around a person in a complicated baby wrap as though the whole endeavor was playtime with a doll. The obsession was close to a middle-school crush: light on the details, heavy on the emotion. For years I had dated the wrong men. Some, I suspect, I chose precisely for their unsuitability. I would not have a child. It could have a disability like my brother's, and I would be stuck. I held my freedom so dear that even a developmentally 'normal' child was too terrifying a prospect. Until it wasn't. As more friends had children, freedom felt less important. I found myself watching television more than venturing out. I was nesting. Suddenly, all previous anxiety surrounding the possibility of a child with a condition like my brother's was gone. It was as though I had never rearranged my entire life around not having a child in the first place.

> **It was as though I had never rearranged my entire life around not having a child in the first place.**

I knew, once I had my own child, I would aspire to being present but not consumed. I had stacked my life so I could *purchase care*. Not a readymade, from a blog or an app, but from other humans. I would go about my day job and occasionally see friends for brunch by utilizing the modern white feminist career ladder outsource-the-rest approach. My emotional reasons for wanting this lifestyle were perhaps more complicated than my peers', given my years of caring for my brother, but by no means unique. Most women I know assumed they would keep their jobs, their Saturday morning yoga, and their friendships. They, however, also aspired to be excellent mothers. Not me. I knew what excellent motherhood required. It took Ukeles having her own child to see what is commonly remarked upon in the media today: women, and especially mothers, bear an outsized amount of the unpaid physical and emotional labor required to run a household. Call it Care. Or *Maintenance Art*. Women are doing it. I did not want to do it. Or I wanted to do it to a lesser degree. I just perhaps stated it differently – I wanted to be an excellent father. I wanted another woman to do the bulk of the care, and I would pick up the fun parts, like an excellent father might. The only way this arrangement would work would be for me to make three to four times what the other woman was paid. And the only way for that to work was for me to do what I did in my twenties and early thirties – play the corporate game.

—

In the past thirty minutes I have twice gone to the next room to pick a monkey doll up from the floor and put it back in my daughter's crib. She needs to learn to stop throwing the monkey out of the crib. I need the wailing to stop so I can edit this paragraph. I need a solution. In 1944, renowned behavioral psychologist B.F. Skinner was expecting his second child. In an effort to 'gadgeteer', or in today's parlance, 'hack', a way to reduce his wife's workload, he invented the baby tender: a temperature-controlled glass box in which the child would spend nearly every waking hour, naked but for a diaper. Horrified parents of the time viewed this as neglect bordering on child abuse, and the boxes never became popular. Skinner's daughter played happily in the baby tender until she was about two. All reports suggest she grew up well-adjusted and lived a normal life. Had a baby tender stopped Josephine from throwing the monkey out of reach, I would have saved ten minutes. Just as Ukeles *gets it*, B.F. Skinner *gets it*, as evidenced in his October 1945 *Ladies Home Journal* article defending his invention (emphasis mine):

> *It is common practice to advise the troubled mother to be patient and tender and to enjoy her baby... But it is the exceptional mother who can fill this prescription upon demand, especially if there are other children in the family and she has no help.* We need to go one step further and treat the mother with affection also. *Simplified childcare will give mother love a chance.*

Had a baby tender stopped Josephine from throwing the monkey out of reach, I would have saved ten minutes.

Many months of Josephine's first year of life were hectic. My husband traveled for work Mondays through Thursdays, leaving me to care for an infant and a slightly wild forty-five-pound dog alone. The dog, a lab-whippet-shepherd-pit mutt we rescued over five years ago, was born at a shelter and adopted and returned four times in her first two years of life. The shelter warned us she may not be good around other dogs, cats, or children. We have poured endless *care* and training into this animal, and in general have been successful. She no longer takes doggy

Prozac. She tolerates Josephine, but she will still eat a cat given the chance, and will pick a fight with other dogs on a walk. She is still, well, wild.

...I felt pressure to rush home to resume the infinite maintenance required of a new mother...

Just as I lacked the time or desire to care for my child 24/7, I paid to send my dog to doggie daycare. Each morning I wrangled my daughter into the baby carrier strapped to my front and made multiple trips from the house to the car. In one hand I carried a bag packed with clothing changes, food, and dog treats, and in the other, coolers and ice packs for breast milk. My abdomen was still weak from a complicated C-section, so avoiding a sidewalk dog fight while walking to the car with an infant strapped to my chest required precision timing and effort. This work and loading of dependents into a vehicle had to be done before 7.45 am, regardless of how much sleep I had gotten. The nanny, Shurrandah, was strict about drop-off times, and I had to rush to arrive on time. My days were full of paid work, grocery shopping, reading about child rearing, and pumping, which is Maintenance to an Art if ever there was. Evening pickups were no better. The dog howled from the anxiety of being left alone in the car and I felt pressure to rush home to resume the infinite maintenance required of a new mother – cooking, cleaning, laundry, bottle washing, night awakenings, breastfeeding, and so on. All of this left me obsessed with how little time

I had, rather than focusing on Shurrandah and her Care of Josephine.

We were delighted to have hired Shurrandah a few months after my daughter was born. She was an expert: an undergraduate degree in childhood education and nineteen-plus years at a daycare. Somewhere along the line I caused a rift in our relationship. I understand now what it was: I relied heavily upon Shurrandah's experience in the first few months, but as time went on, I gained my footing as a mother and turned more to peers, pediatricians, and data to make parenting decisions. She insisted Josephine wear hard-soled shoes indoors; I maintained my stance that she wear soft slippers. The other nanny-share family had the advantage of spending leisure time with Shurrandah at their house. My conversations were little more than a quick, 'How are you? Here are some extra diapers. Should I bring more milk?' before I had to head out. She required more. Shurrandah was a few years older than me, childless, and going through a divorce. Eventually she revealed that she was tired of taking care of other people's children. Add to this the racial and socio-economic dynamics at play (both employer families were white, she was Black), and of course she became offended by my daily refusal to purchase my daughter shoes. But even deeper than any of this, I suspect her expertise felt threatened, her Art not appreciated. I fear I left Shurrandah with the impression she was little more than a glorified version of Skinner's baby tender. In not

wanting, rightly or not, to take care of my brother
during my teens and twenties, I had developed
not just an aversion to Care, but to those who
performed the Care as well.

—

Josephine is supposed to be napping, once again,
but she has taken off her sleep sack and clothing. I
do not know how Skinner's baby tender prevented
his daughter from ripping off her diaper, but at
least it kept her warm. I suspect Shurrandah would
never have tolerated the ripping off of diapers. In
my husband's absence, I did rely upon her for many
things. She taught my daughter to hold her own
bottle and sent us tutorials on feeding oatmeal.
When I arrived frazzled and late, I would often
complain about my husband – another early Friday
meeting prevented him, yet again, from dropping
her off. Shurrandah loved my husband and often
suggested that I ease up on him. I was constantly
told I had brought the wrong cup and Josephine's
clothing didn't match. My husband's absence made
him an excellent parent; my terseness made me
a horrible mother. Shurrandah deserved more
respect. I deserved more respect. Skinner's baby
tender deserved more respect. Throughout, I held
fast to my aspiration to be an excellent father,
permission only I can grant.

    I am writing this during the pandemic. We
took Josephine out of the nanny share in our
Washington, DC neighborhood, instead choosing

to drive five days across the country to stay with my in-laws in Montana. The decision seemed rational at the time. There was a pandemic, and a cocooned household would be safer. I was having conflicts with Shurrandah, and my mother-in-law, who adores children, volunteered to watch Josephine half days while I drastically reduced my

**I can do this while washing dishes.
Perhaps this makes it Art.
Perhaps this makes it bearable.**

workload. This may have been a miscalculation. Montana is lovely. Yes, we can go hiking and gaze at mountains, but in addition to joining the millions of other mothers who have cut back on paid work, I am constantly forced into maintenance work not of my choosing. I prefer to sleep in sheets that could be washed and find my jeans on a chair rather than spend precious seconds maintaining a semblance of order. My thoughts I want free of what Ukeles calls 'noodiling [sic] maintenance'. I think this is what we are currently calling 'emotional labor' – all the thought and preparation that goes into everyday tasks. Which soap is best or cheapest? What should we have for dinner tonight, tomorrow, every night for the rest of our lives? Do we have enough paper towels? Should I watch a reality television show about how to organize my closets? I do not want to fill my head with such things. Instead, I want to listen to a podcast about theosophy, its connection to New Age movements and to the Indian independence movement. I can do this while washing dishes. Perhaps this makes it Art. Perhaps this makes it bearable.

Having this luxury, this privilege, to spend half my days volunteering with the election and the other half caring for my daughter, is not lost on me. Yet still I struggle, because this is not how I want to spend my time. I struggle because feminizing and equalizing a household of perfectly content seventy-five-year-olds is proving difficult. No matter the suggestions I make, the roles I divvy up, I still find my mother-in-law cooking as my father-in-law reads, out loud, an article detailing the saga of a Komodo dragon undergoing cataract surgery at an Ohio zoo. Meanwhile my husband works around the

...what gives me the right to put women of color at physical risk when I can isolate my child and our family can still make rent?

clock. The inequity irks me. But then, the seeming inequity of having to care for my own daughter irked me. The inequity of handing my child to a Black or brown woman for low wages irks me. On Nextdoor, a hyperlocal social media platform, people were calling out nannies for gathering in parks and not wearing masks. To this a Black woman posted repeatedly: WATCH YOUR OWN CHILDREN. I understand her point, especially now – what gives me the right to put women of color at physical risk when I can isolate my child and our family can still make rent? But is that the answer; that we all homestead in earth ships made of recycled bottles and grow our own food? It seems unlikely. But now, after ~~eight nine~~ ten months of watching my own child in some form or fashion, it is jarring to think that another person cared for her so intimately and for so many hours of each day. It is equally jarring to consider that I did anything else. When would I have showered, exercised, napped, talked with friends, or tended to myself?

—

This essay is nearly finished, but rather than completing it tomorrow, I fear my free time will be spent purchasing stamps for holiday cards and ordering presents. In one parent (read: mom) Facebook group I am part of, women continue to ask how other mothers are watching or schooling their children and keeping their jobs. One woman posted: 'The "hack" as it were, has always been working while others care for our kids, in the hopes that in being ambitious and productive we will be fuller humans and ultimately better mothers in the long term.' This woman *gets it*. There is no hack. Skinner and his wife were complete lunatics if they kept a nineteen-month-old in a baby tender all day. Children this age have to run and move and explore their bodies and surroundings. No app, no readymade, and no baby tender can solve my quandary. Perhaps there is something comforting in the fact that we have not found a substitute for the human element.

I have recently been suffering from bouts of insomnia. I wake up at 2 am and won't fall asleep again until 5 am. My thoughts turn to how much caretaking I have to do the next day. Last night the dog crawled into my bed. In the middle of my insomnia, she scrabbled her paws on my legs, chasing her dream prey. It made me consider that the only way to care for myself, the one element missing from all this Art, was to live a life alone, single in an apartment with my books and my thoughts as I had in my twenties in New York when I actively ran from caring for others. The dog, the husband, the house, the child – it all was too much. I snapped at the poor sleeping animal for keeping me awake. I realized it wasn't her fault and felt bad about yelling at her. I curled my knees into her back and nestled my head near her face and quickly fell asleep. Caring, ironically, was the only thing to release me from my care-induced anxiety.

I have come to both revile and revere Maintenance.

Caring, ironically, was the only thing to release me from my care-induced anxiety.

As much as I am impatient for an end to the pandemic and for a day when I can safely hand Josephine to someone else, this pause has given me an in-depth opportunity to reflect on what it means to Care, and what caring could look like. I do not think I can emotionally accept the idea that the laundry will never be done. I do not know how to intellectually reconcile that I never noticed when laundry was filthy when I was in my twenties. Had you asked me then to turn my chores into Art, I may have considered it briefly, then countered that there were better ways to do Art. This, I think, remains my truth today. In the end, it is neither fully drudgery nor Art. These acts are both drudgery and Art. The reverence is in the dung; it is the cost of doing business, shall we say. If you want a child, you wipe a bottom. If you want an Earth, you clean its air; a Republic, you vote; a city, you repair its bridges; a community, you communicate. And while I can hold these tensions in opposition, I cannot completely turn my Maintenance, my caregiving, into Art. But I cannot honestly and fully give it to another woman – paid or unpaid – in the current care economy. I cannot *not* give it to another woman, at the risk of hollowing out my own soul. I cannot *not* view my life as Art, and this is not my chosen Art. When this pandemic ends, when we return to Washington, DC, I will be putting Josephine in full-time daycare. She should be with people who have chosen to spend their days with toddlers, not with a mother who is mentally attending to other passions. In the end the only solution seems an obvious one: make caregiving a true Art, an exalted profession. Let the women and men for whom this is a passion be paid generously for their time, their expertise, their ability to entertain a toddler for six, seven, eight hours a day. Free me from the mental gymnastics of this conceptual Art. ◨

To:

remain.

by Zachary D. Shell

The young man paces outside the auditorium, swallowing the evening's fresh spring air. He hears the principal's voice on the microphone inside and looks at the arch overhead. Relaxes his grip on the rolled-up program in his hand. Footsteps approach, and he turns: a classmate races past and applause spills out as the auditorium door swings open; as the principal calls his classmates' names; as the young man's grip tightens again on the program, fingers leaving indentations on its glossy sheen. He feels his pulse quicken – feels his tie, too tight around his neck; his shoes, too stiff. He pulls out his headphones and finds his song. Presses play. *Looks like nothing's gonna change.* Pulse slowing again. *Everything still remains the same.* Phone buzzing, but he ignores it. *I can't do what ten people tell me to do.* The principal is calling his own name now, but the young man doesn't hear it. *So I guess I'll remain the same.* He drops the program in the trash and takes one final glance at the arch. This is what it looks like to cross the threshold. What it looks like to stop compromising, to finally say 'enough.'

To: remain.

There is a boy, years younger than the young man. He's sitting outside a cottage on a Vermont summer night, ten miles from the camp he deserted that afternoon; sitting in his pajamas as the radio plays softly behind him — ashamed of the camp uniform now lying discarded on the floor. The boy pushes his feet off the ground and feels the rocking chair shift with the rhythm of the voice — sounding anguished and weary, and singing the same song he'll listen to outside the auditorium six years later. But the boy doesn't know it. This boy will become that young man — looking up at the arch and reaching for his headphones — but he wouldn't recognize his older self. He hasn't learned that young men pace outside of auditoriums, that they finally say 'enough.' He doesn't know that he himself —

is back in his seat in suburban New Jersey: Senior Awards Night at Princeton High School, one hour before walking out — one hour before finally saying 'enough.' The young man watches the principal read names into the microphone, watches his classmates cross the stage for a handshake and a plaque. This young man, watching from the crowd: suffocating in his tie and longing for the fresh air on the other side of the arch. He doesn't want to be in this auditorium – three weeks from graduation and desperate to leave – but his mom told him to go; his mom told him to go, but he knows he won't be receiving an award because he's still the same boy he was six years earlier. The boy outside the cottage on a Vermont summer night. The boy who –

doesn't win awards either. Even the Monopoly game lies unfinished and abandoned – exposing his shame like the pleading letter he sent home earlier that week, like his mother picking him up in the camp office and taking him away. The boy clutches his knees and does the math in his head: two months until school begins, eleven months until another summer; still the same boy, and the clock is ticking to become a better version. Six years later, he'll cross a different threshold – back out under the arch – but tonight he's still compromising; tonight, he doesn't know anything else. He doesn't know that half a century earlier, another young man – the same young man now singing on the radio; a young man who was tired of compromising, who finally said 'enough' – sat on the dock of the bay and decided

To: remain.

—

Otis Redding's road to the San Francisco Bay begins in Macon, Georgia, where the son of a deacon learns that life won't be entirely his to live. Otis grows up singing in his father's church.

His voice is a source of pride for the old man; his turn away from the choir, one of disappointment – turning instead towards the jazz and blues clubs downtown. Despite his father's opposition, Otis quickly makes a name for himself: his bravado attracting women far too old for him; himself growing too old, too soon. Soon, he's fronting a local band called the Pinetoppers. Soon, he's the biggest draw in town. And soon – 1960 – eighteen-year-old Otis heads to Los Angeles to try his luck.

Otis, who left his home in Georgia only to return; whose loneliness already won't leave him alone

Otis misses his mark in California: plays a few gigs, but he never catches on; makes a few records, but he can't catch a break. It isn't long before cracks start to show in his conviction. 'Otis thought he should be in the big town,' his agent, Alex Hodges, recalls, 'but he learned he wasn't cut out for it,'[1] and the following summer the young man packs it in: back to his wife, Zelma, and the birth of their first child –

Otis, who left his home in Georgia only to return; whose loneliness already won't leave him alone.

—

The boy remembers camp the year before: feeling nervous on the first day and shrinking inside his Ghostbusters shirt; standing in the corner until Owen said, 'Cool shirt!' – then Cam: 'Yeah, cool shirt!' – then all three, finding their cabin together. Later, the director welcomed the boys to the start of summer, to all the hiking and archery and canoeing. And the director: proud of the men those boys would become, excited for the badges they'd earn. But then he took out his songbook, and the boy couldn't believe there was singing besides all the hiking and archery and canoeing; singing while everyone else was silent – mouthing the lyrics and looking for distractions – but Owen was yelping and Cam was laughing, and the three together: how great to be singing at summer camp. These three together, with the boy who knew nothing about loneliness or the cottage porch, who felt nothing like –

the young man in the auditorium, envying the students in the spotlight and loathing his own anonymity. He went to a few parties like he was supposed to but preferred being home; joined a few clubs like he was supposed to but preferred being alone; tried to be more like everyone else but always felt most comfortable as himself – unremarkable and undistinguished, unable to become someone new. He shrinks into his seat as his classmates' accomplishments flash on the screen behind them, each biography dissolving into a blurry mess of yearbook superlatives: most likely to succeed, nicest smile, most popular. Least likely to have left summer camp –

four days after scratching out his pleading midnight letter; after receiving a different letter from Owen and Cam before summer even began: *We're not moving into the next age group.* Just the boy moving up alone, but there were no Ghostbusters shirts on the older side of camp – just the uniform: too proper, too stuffy. Another welcome dinner, and the boy sat quietly: staring into his mashed potatoes while his bunkmates bragged about hiking and archery and canoeing, waiting for the director to pull out his songbook – but this year no one else sang. Then quickly, the boy was mouthing the words and looking for distractions. Straightening his tie. Smoothing his sleeves. But he heard the snickering and knew he had revealed himself. And the boy understood – even though some things never change – that summer camp was one thing that already had.

—

The deacon is waiting when Otis returns from Los Angeles – warning his son that his career will flop and promising to never watch him perform. Johnny Jenkins is waiting, too: the new star of the downtown clubs, rising to the top in Otis' absence. He books the biggest gigs in town while the young man toils away in the dives.

February 1962: Johnny Jenkins gets an audition with Stax Records, and Otis drives him to Memphis – but it's Otis, pleading for the final take of the session; Otis, taking one shot with 'These Arms of Mine'; and Otis, later that year, with the first hit single of his career. Now Otis: naive and ambitious and desperate for his father's affirmation. He blindly signs the first contract Stax offers, inadvertently surrendering the royalties for his entire future catalog.

Nevertheless, the Stax deal is Otis' breakthrough. He begins touring with Booker T. & the M.G.'s, but keyboardist Dennis Wheeler remembers him as 'the type of guy who had a million acquaintances and few real friends.'[2] There are even fewer on the road, so Otis is back home whenever he can – hosting barbecues and hunting trips, recording demos at the old studio. Familiar comforts for a young man who feels himself slipping away.

—

The young man is not without his own modest success ... but even these are reminders of his ordinariness

The young man is not without his own modest success: twice-a-year choir concerts and ensemble parts in the annual musical – but even these are reminders of his ordinariness. Always just a face in the crowd. Then, this year, his big break: playing the second lead, the comic relief; feeling vindicated with his face pulled out of the crowd, but still only the face of a buffoon – the bumbling fool begging for laughs. He went to school the next day and walked past the promotional poster, proud of his picture in the center and his name in bold. He heard the whispers – 'this is him?' – and that *was* him, the young man, but everyone else just saw the buffoon: now sitting in the auditorium on Awards Night, wishing for one more opportunity to become someone spectacular – wondering about some other world where unspectacular young men are exactly who they're supposed to be. Unlike the real world, where he's still the boy –

who learned long before the cottage porch that being himself wasn't enough. Middle school orientation, two months after his first summer at camp: the boy, searching for friends amongst unfamiliar faces; his friends, sitting at a table full of them – unfamiliar faces wearing polo shirts, and his friends in polo, too. The boy glanced down at his Ghostbusters shirt, wondering what happened to *theirs*, wondering when he was supposed to change. The principal said to find a seat, but everywhere the boy looked were unfamiliar faces and polo shirts and – there – the table in the corner: other students who hadn't spent that summer becoming someone new, still wearing Barbie shirts and G.I. Joe hats and plastic stick-on earrings. Not noticing when he sat down. And the principal: 'Welcome to middle school,' but the boy felt the roof caving in; 'Enjoy these next few years,' but the boy knew better – knew that sixth graders like him sat at the corner table and blended into the wall, that they buried their shame in their laps. He knew he'd still be sitting at that corner table when sixth grade ended; knew he'd still be himself, knew it still wouldn't be enough. *Looks like nothing's gonna change.* He knew he'd still be –

sick of shame and disappointment, longing for that other world where he's exactly who he's supposed to be. But there *is* no other world – only the one where he's still his same damn self, so tonight the young man wants validation in this world instead: proof that someone noticed. He flips through the program and checks the back; turns it over, turns it upside down. Nothing.

—

November 1963: Apollo Theater, Harlem. The nation's top soul acts come together for a week-long showcase, and Otis is the rookie in a field of veterans. Ben E. King describes him before the first set 'sweating and trembling, worrying about his suit, his voice, the band, everything,'[3] but the young man lives up to the billing – commanding the stage and leaving Jerry Wexler, president of Atlantic Records, to remark simply, 'Otis was magic.' But Wexler detects his vulnerability as well. 'You could feel this plea… that covered every song he sang.'[4]

The Apollo makes Otis a star. Eager to break into the mainstream, Stax begins sending him to clubs where Black singers have never performed, in cities the young man has never visited. Alex Hodges remembers, 'The sense that this guy had to be seen to be believed was building every day,'[5] but Otis grows no more comfortable in the rock circuit, no more comfortable on the road; no less homesick for his family, so he buys three hundred acres in the Georgia countryside and builds the Big O Ranch. He discovers the most secure version of himself – homebody Otis, country boy Otis – but his records keep selling and he's rarely home anyway. Traveling all over the country. Doing whatever Stax tells him to do.

September 1966: London, England. Two weeks filling auditoriums, two weeks electrifying the crowds. Stax capitalizes immediately – now marketing Otis as an international superstar – but the young man's contradictions continue to consume him: his charisma on stage masking his anxiety in the spotlight, his savvy charm betrayed by discomfort with his own fame. Stax president Al Bell recalls of Otis' swelling confidence, 'That was in many ways a front.'[6]

> **The young man's contradictions continue to consume him: his charisma on stage masking his anxiety in the spotlight**

June 1967: Monterey Music Festival. Otis is the headliner, but Zelma has never seen her husband so distressed – just two months back from his second European tour and apprehensive about facing the hippie crowd. He wants to stay home – to finally say 'enough' – but Stax needs their biggest star to hook another audience. 'Oh, God, yes, I wanted him to go,' Al Bell admits. 'Man, he had to go.'[7] And Dennis Wheeler remembers the young man: Otis, loyal to a fault. He can't say no.[8]

Now: more time away from a family growing used to his absence.

—

The boy had wanted to stay home that summer. Humiliated after sixth grade and disappointed by his friends' letter, but his mom said camp would be good for him: after all, boys like camp, and this boy was supposed to like it, too. Hiking, archery, canoeing. Preparing for the midsummer talent contest, but his bunkmates needed a third for basketball – and since no other world exists, the

John was the star, Kevin was the sidekick, and the boy stood next to the sideline – trying to stay invisible until the ball rolled to his feet

boy wanted validation in this world instead. In this world: John was the star, Kevin was the sidekick, and the boy stood next to the sideline – trying to stay invisible until the ball rolled to his feet. He picked it up and took two dribbles. Launched a shot and watched it go in. And the boy felt vindicated as John ran towards him: shock on the star's face and arm held high in the air, but the boy acted too excited – wound up for a high-five like he'd never made a basket before. Then John: lowering his arm and turning away, shaking his head at Kevin. Then the boy:

    – panic –

        – what? –

Humiliated again. Feet frozen to the court. And he knew this was one opportunity he'd never get back, that he was exactly who he always was: not the star, not the sidekick – just the boy who high-fives wrong. The game continued: stomach churning as the ball rolled to his feet, but this time the boy passed it back. The summer continued, and he still craved validation; still did what his bunkmates told him to do; still wound up on this cottage porch anyway – walking right back into the familiar world of corner tables and shame, wrong shirts and wrong high-fives. *Everything still remains the same.* More disappointment for the boy who six years later –

is imagining some overlooked acknowledgment: his name on the microphone, his biography on the screen, affirmation of the person he wanted to become. Suddenly, his mom whispers that he'll be receiving an award after all, chosen for his participation that year in a peer mentorship program. Fourteen students in the group, but only one receiving recognition: a concession to his conformity. The young man glances through the program again – how did he miss his name? – but his mom whispers:
'It's not in there.'

– panic –

   – *what?* –

Mom: 'Don't worry, they said they would call you up anyway.' But the young man looks at the students on stage and knows that she's arranged it – summoning him from the crowd as an afterthought. He knows he's not the leader this second-wave celebration says he is: no different now than the previous evening or the one before, no closer to being anyone else than the last time his mom saved him – six years earlier, picking him up from summer camp and bringing him to that cottage in Vermont.

And now the young man is his younger self again: the boy on the porch, the boy at the corner table, the boy who high-fived wrong. The boy with the loneliness that wouldn't leave him alone.

—

Otis is a hit at Monterey. Phil Walden, founder of Capricorn Records, recalls, 'He knew from the get-go he had 'em,'[9] and the young man doesn't let up – plowing through his set and delivering what critic Jon Landau would describe as 'the highest level of expression rock 'n' roll has yet attained.'[10] Otis leaves the festival with his throat inflamed, his voice reduced to a whisper. He needs time to recover, but Stax isn't satisfied: now sending him back on tour up the California coast. Farther from his home in Georgia. Heading for the 'Frisco Bay.

Looks like nothing's gonna change.

Otis is pulled in three directions after Monterey: Stax, still looking for a crossover hit, pressuring their biggest star to write a folk song for a counterculture ravenous for more of him; the Black national consciousness, rising in sophistication, turning away from a Southern soul man too backwater for his own good; and Otis himself – clinging to his roots and waiting for something to come his way.

Everything still remains the same.

Now the road that first left Macon seven years earlier is arriving in San Francisco, but those closest to Otis sense a change: a new resolve from this young man who's tired of touring, tired of compromising, tired of that damn loneliness that still won't leave him alone. He rents a houseboat and sits each morning on the dock of the bay, watching the ships and writing his final testimony: the plea of a young man who's tired, too, of a life not entirely his to live – who never knew what kind of life he should be living instead.

I can't do what ten people tell me to do.

When Zelma hears the final recording, Otis' voice will sound like a siren – a familiar cry at an unexpected volume. 'It seems,' she'll later say, 'as though the song was letting you know, "I won't be here a long, long time."'[11]

So I guess I'll remain the same.

—

The boy thinks something is wrong with him. He knows he shouldn't be sad, shouldn't be lonely. He knows boys shouldn't be picked up from summer camp two weeks too early, and he knows nothing's going to change because nothing *has* changed; knows no other world exists, so he'll have to change instead – transforming into the seventh-grader he's supposed to be, the type of camper he should have already become. He doesn't know there's another option, that young men don't always become who they're supposed to be. *I can't do what ten people tell me to do.* He doesn't know that he'll become a young man –

who's tired of the charade, tired of following the script – never imagining his turn in the spotlight would turn into another moment of shame. Tired of being unspectacular, of only being himself, but tonight he's that soul man on the radio, and it's his own voice coming through the window: 'Enough.' The principal returns to the microphone to present the next award, but the young man doesn't notice. He checks for his headphones. He rolls up the program. Under the arch, out the door, across the threshold. He has finally decided

To: remain.

———

Otis Redding records '(Sittin' On) The Dock of the Bay' on December 7, 1967. Three days later, he'll be dead.

Fifty-four years later: my mind turns to a boy sitting outside a cottage in rural Vermont, to a young man pacing outside an auditorium in suburban New Jersey. Those two look familiar. They look like ghosts from the past.

I look at that young man, and I'm as shocked to see him from this vantage point as I would've been six years earlier in Vermont. I remember his tie, too tight; his shoes, too stiff. I remember his resentment after so many years of disappointment;

his disappointment, winding up exactly as himself. And yet, I can't recall ever feeling as confident as he did on Awards Night – walking away from the validation he craved, trusting that the best version of himself wasn't the one inscribed on his plaque.

Whenever I think about myself outside the auditorium, I'm reminded of another young man who took the world as he found it

He thought he was crossing a threshold that evening; for the most part, he was right. Most days, I'm comfortable facing the world as the young man I can't avoid being, but part of me is still the boy on the cottage porch – longing for whoever I might have been in some other world. My younger self couldn't have known his choices would define him, but at what point is a boy who hates summer camp allowed to accept who he is? How long does he owe it to himself to change? Does he ever? That boy doesn't need forgiveness for taking the world as he found it; the young man doesn't, either. I just wish they knew it wouldn't always be easy on the other side of the arch.

Whenever I think about myself outside the auditorium, I'm reminded of another young man who took the world as he found it – who spent too long compromising just to become someone spectacular. But then I see that other young man on the dock, see him deciding – trusting – that the best version of himself wasn't the one Stax or his father or the Black community told him to be. I see him declare that simply being Otis was enough.

I see him in the morning sun, but if I look closer I can make out the boy still inside: too young for so much responsibility and burden. I recognize that boy's desperation. I recognize his disappointment. I hear him through the ears of the boy on the cottage porch, and his voice doesn't sound as celebratory anymore – it sounds like a confession that he could never become who he was supposed to be, like resignation: anguished and weary. I hear Otis as I did on that Vermont summer evening, and I ache for the young man who roamed two thousand miles just to make that dock his home. I wonder if he knew it wouldn't always be easy on the other side of the bay.

Now taking off. Now coming back down. Crashing into Wisconsin's Lake Monona. Otis: gone

I see him crossing a threshold, but there's one final part to this story: the winter morning, three days after leaving Stax studios for the final time; the midwest sky threatening overhead; and Otis, anxious to make it to a gig in Madison, asking his pilot if he can fly the little Beechcraft plane safely. Now taking off. Now coming back down. Crashing into Wisconsin's Lake Monona.

Otis: gone.

—

I pace outside the auditorium, swallowing the evening's fresh spring air. A classmate races past and the principal calls another name. My grip tightens again on the rolled-up program in my hand. I pull out my headphones and find my song. Press play. Phone buzzing, but I ignore it as Otis' voice floods my ears, as the young man sings through the bridge – his words steadying me. The voice fades, and I remove my headphones; drop the program in the trash and take one final glance at the arch. Otis didn't get enough time, but the rest of mine still lies ahead. So I guess I'll remain the same. ∎

1   Ribowsky, Mark. *Dreams to Remember: Otis Redding, Stax Records, and the Transformation of Southern Soul.* Liveright Publishing Corporation (2016), p54.
2   Ribowsky, p. 96
3   'Throwback 1963: Otis Redding Debuts at the Apollo.' *SoulMusic*, www.soulmusic. com/article/throwback-1963-otis-redding-debuts-apollo. Accessed 3 Feb. 2022.
4   Wexler, Jerry, and David Ritz. *Rhythms and Blues: A Life in American Music.* Knopf (1993), p196.
5   Ribowsky, p110
6   Ribowsky, p159
7   Ribowsky, p226
8   Ribowsky, p220
9   Phil Walden interview, *Monterey Pop Festival.*
10 Guralnick, Peter. *Sweet Soul Music: Rhythm and Blues and the Southern Dream of Freedom.* Back Bay Books (1999), p320–321.
11 Bynum, Ross. 'Otis Redding Still Drawing Fans.' *AP NEWS*, 5 Dec. 1997, apnews. com/article/a14f55f7b1c9377c5a8cb218528163b4.

LONDON LIT LAB

Online courses in 2022, for beginner to advanced writers:

- Self-Adaptation: Making the Personal Publishable
- Art of Play: Enhancing your Flash Fiction
- Freeing your Voice: Reclaiming the Inner Writer
- Short Story Bootcamp: Fix, Polish, Submit!
- Creative Nonfiction: Compelling Memoir
- Saltwater Folk Tales
- and many more!

Or join a **Live Online** masterclass, including:

- The Novella-in-Flash: How to Get Started (and Keep Going) with Michael Loveday

Join our community and nurture your talent in a supportive environment with like-minded people, where writers teach writers.

'Lily and Zoe offer teaching and coaching at the highest level. Their workshops have a reputation for encouraging excellence and creativity in a supportive environment. I am always recommending them.' Julia Bell, Course Convenor, MA Creative Writing, Birkbeck.

www.londonlitlab.co.uk

2022 QUEEN MARY WASAFIRI

NEW WRITING PRIZE

Judged by Mary Jean Chan, Marina Salandy-Brown, Preti Taneja, and Francesca Wade

___

£1,000

and mentoring for Fiction, Life Writing, and Poetry

OPEN JAN - JUNE 2022

wasafiri.org/new-writing-prize

Wasafiri · Queen Mary University of London · Routledge Taylor & Francis Group · TLC The Literary Consultancy · THE GOOD LITERARY AGENCY

Wee Kenny: Poete Maudit

by Rob McClure Smith

Whenever asked to name a significant influence on my writing, I usually say: 'Kenneth Bianchi.' Most people don't know who that is. A few will say: 'Really? The infamous serial killer, kidnapper and rapist also known as the Hillside Strangler and suspect in the so-called Alphabet Murders?' To them, I say: 'No, not that Kenneth Bianchi. Another one. And how come you know so much about serial killers? What's the matter with you? Are you sick?'

The Kenneth Bianchi I admire as a writer never actually wrote anything. He may well have been functionally illiterate. Kenny was more of an oral poet, like Homer (and Ossian), and also, like many a superhero of note, unaware of his hidden powers. Let me begin with a sample of his early, more primitive work while still a poetic *ephebe*.

I. Theft

It was 1977, the year of punk, and approaching 5th November, the biggest night of the year on a West of Scotland council housing estate. This was Guy Fawkes Night when us schemies erected and burnt elaborate and architecturally complex bonfires and became these insane incendiaries for a night, inadvertently torching entire neighborhoods.

It took at least two weeks to steal enough material to construct the perfect bonfire. This period was a veritable nightmare for nearby workplaces that couldn't leave anything remotely flammable lying around lest it disappeared pronto. When the employees of a local abattoir left their huge sausage tables outside to dry during their lunch hour, a team of us crawled through the tall grass in the fashion of Viet Cong guerillas during the Tet offensive, sprinted across a patio strewn with blood and flecks of viscera, hoisted up a few of those unwieldy scaffoldings, and staggered off with them. These tables were about the size of gallows, and heavier. I still wonder at the expressions of those workers upon their return to the slaughterhouse only to discover that their enormous worktables had somehow suddenly vanished into thin air. It must have had the quality of an alien abduction.

By 4th November, we had run out of obvious things to pilfer and, clad in anarchist black, raided local lumberyards under cover of darkness. One night, while being pursued by a security guard and his vicious Alsatian, a group of us bolted across a busy intersection. Gordon 'Go-Go' Walker almost got sideswiped by a milk truck and in his panic, dropped a few planks of fresh-cut lumber behind him on the road.

'Don't leave that there,' Kenny yelled at him, annoyed. 'Wood doesn't grow on trees.' It was a memorable line of superb verse. That was the thing about Kenny. His best poetic work was, unbeknownst to him, often perfect in rhythm and meter. Also, equally unbeknownst to him, it was terrifically funny.

His best poetic work was, unbeknownst to him, often perfect in rhythm and meter

Other friends knew when they were being funny. Take 'Go-Go' Walker as an example. It was Go-Go who suggested we steal coffins from a nearby coffin-maker for the base of our pyramidal bonfire. And it was Go-Go who rescued one of the coffins from the conflagration so he could put wheels on it and construct what he called the perfect Go-Go cart. But this was also, I realise in retrospect, just so he could yell at another friend, David 'Doc' Morrison, while riding his remarkable macabre vehicle down Stonefield Street: 'Hey, Doc, can you give me something to stop my coffin?'

You could never repeat Kenny's best lines in front of him, because he'd get angry, and he had much the same demeanor and temper as Joe Pesci in *Goodfellas*. It was when he wasn't around that his classic lines became an integral part of our street patter. We'd be standing in a close mouth, smoking Woodbines, checking out the local talent, and someone would say: 'Wee Kenny says he's going to get off with that Sandra McNamee at the Countdown disco this Friday night.' There'd be a pause and then someone else would note *sotto voce*: 'Aye, and wood doesn't grow on trees.'

II. Assault

I do Kenny a disservice. On one occasion I recall him being intentionally funny, perfecting his poetic art with a deadpan accuracy. He and I used to walk to high school together, which was a hazardous business then. We attended a nondenominational institution. But it didn't matter how many Muslims or Mormons or Hindus or Jehovah's Witnesses or Jews attended, we knew what it was: the Protestant school. We were made to wear these grotesque uniforms: grey pants, blue tie with yellow stripes, and bright blue blazer with Academy badge. Blue was a Protestant color, the color of a Glasgow Rangers strip (no Catholic was ever good enough to play for them). Blue was the trim of the Orange sashes swaying down High Street on 12th July (each toss of the stick and smack of the lambeg signifying the buggering of the Pope). Walking to the Protestant school through a predominantly Catholic area was the equivalent of donning a billboard designed by Jasper Johns. In the West of Scotland, in working class neighborhoods, *grogging* on those of the 'other persuasion' was SOP. Catholics, if in the majority, spat on Protestants: Protestants, if numerically superior, spat on Catholics. It was just the way things were then, a reciprocal arrangement, spitting was our way of transgressing the sectarian divide. Sometimes you were unlucky due to an accident of geography. I walked to school most mornings, head slunk against a Catholic deluge, this tsunami of spit flying at me. I wasn't personally to blame for the Reformation, but some days it felt like I was.

My father, a serious drinker and bigot, was not enthused by the condition of my blazer and made it known there would be consequences. So, either I could fight back against the spitters (and so get myself bludgeoned by mobs of irate Fenians, my own personal auto-de-fe) or march relentlessly through that wall of sputum, as placid as Gandhi, to get seriously whipped by my father when I got home. You might say I was on the horns of a dilemma in trying to maintain the condition of that damn blazer. But it was not to be, and it wasn't the Catholics who finished it off either.

This particular day, Kenny and I and Go-Go were accompanied to school by Doc. Doc was from the neighborhood, but his parents had serious pretensions. They actually had him learn a musical instrument, the violin of all things. There's only one thing worse than being seen carrying a violin case through a council estate – and that's being seen with someone carrying a violin case through a council estate. My usual strategy on espying Doc's approach, instrument in hand, was to throw my hands in the air and yell 'don't shoot.' I deployed said strategy on this occasion and Doc, irritated, was having none of it. We were passing a bakery at the time, one inexplicably adjacent to the abattoir (it was all very Glasgow). Someone had dropped one of the bakery's more unfortunate confections, a big strawberry trifle, on the pavement, and left it there to rot. Even the birds expressed no interest in that hideous concoction; sparrows aren't stupid. It wasn't that the trifle was inedible from being on the ground, it had been inedible all along. A trifle is truly a terrible thing, a dessert made with fruit, a thin layer of sponge fingers soaked in sherry, smothered in yellow custard, topped with slick whipped cream. The fruit and sponge are suspended in four layers of quivering red jelly, with smudges of chocolate and coffee eerily mixed into its unpleasant blancmange-like texture. It's nothing at all like devil's cake, but it is like something Satan would eat.

A trifle is truly a terrible thing, a dessert made with fruit, a thin layer of sponge fingers soaked in sherry, smothered in yellow custard, topped with slick whipped cream

Doc stood over this dead trifle, clutching his violin case to his side, staring at me malignantly. 'I'm going to kick this at you,' he said in a monotone. I laughed. I was standing thirty feet away. Good luck with that mate. Anyway, he'd never try it. Then he tried it. I'd played soccer with Doc. He wasn't a good player, but a vicious thug, with a kick like a mule. We had this joke that, one night, Doc came home after an especially brutal game with a badly bruised leg and his mother took a look at it and said, 'That's terrible, son' and Doc replied, 'Aye, and I don't even know whose it is.' Anyway, Doc booted that trifle at me like Johann Cruyff and the thing screamed through the air like a Scud missile with this incredible velocity, detaching from its plastic container en route, rotating like a whirligig and, as I ducked, taking necessary evasive action – and failing – it smacked me right in the kisser. I stood there, stunned, looking like a clown in the circus, smears of custard dripping down my cheeks and all this strawberry icing stuck in my hair. The layers of sponge and gelatin had exploded all over the blazer, which somewhat resembled a Jackson Pollock painting. I could barely see, at least until I slowly extracted layers of thick whipped cream out of my eye sockets.

I stood there, stunned, looking like a clown in the circus, smears of custard dripping down my cheeks and all this strawberry icing stuck in my hair

As I did so, I saw the look of mingled amazement and horror on Doc's face; Go-Go literally lying in a gutter, incapable of reassembling his limbs as he laughed in a hysterical frenzy; and wee Kenny beside me, perusing my thoroughly ruined blazer and shaking his head sorrowfully, declaring: 'Wee Rab, not a man to be *trifled* with.'

'Shut the fuck up,' I suggested.

Kenny sighed. 'I suppose this would be your just *desserts*.'

III. Murder

Kenny dropped out of school at 16 after a unfortunate incident involving the Bunting brothers. The Buntings were this extended family of lunatic dwarves who terrorized our school. Kenny crossed them by making a crack about Christmas elves. It did not go down well. Neither did Kenny when a coterie of these Buntings crammed him into a metal dustbin, screwed the lid on, and threw him off a railway bridge into the Monklands canal. Kenny survived, pretty much, but decided education was not for him.

Many years passed. I accidentally ended up living in the United States. I hadn't been back in Scotland for years, and then my father died. For the first time in a decade, I was in my old scheme to break up the council flat and sell the furniture. On my way over to the chippies after the funeral – for I suddenly craved Irn Bru, as one does after a family bereavement – a familiar figure, albeit now sporting a buzz cut, roared by on a motorcycle. The bike did a 360 and pulled up beside me.

'Wee Rab,' the biker said, laughing. 'What do you get when you cross a Glasgow Celtic supporter with a pig?'

'I don't know, Kenny.'

'I don't either. See, there are some things even a pig just won't do. Haw haw.'

We decided for nostalgia's sake to down a few lagers at the Boar's Head, a famed local watering hole of our misspent youth. It was the kind of place where you could spit on the floor (like it was a Catholic) and no one cared. We had been drinking there since we were fifteen. Like I said, no one cared. Honestly, I was relieved we were just drinking, suspecting Kenny might have become a skinhead in the interim and fearing he was about to propose we stop by a National Front rally, or some such. Instead, I told him all about my life in Massachusetts. He was interested in my observation that it was possible to 'pull chicks' there merely by exaggerating your Scottish accent. I was working on adding a speech impediment to sound more like Sean Connery.

'You look nothing like big Sean though, Rab. You've no build,' Kenny noted with disdain. 'You look like a fucking scarecrow got caught in a wind tunnel.'

'Yes, well…'"

'You look like a good fart would blow you away.'

'Yes,' I said. 'I know. I already agreed with you, in advance.'

It was Kenny I wanted to hear more about. I was intrigued to see how his poetic skills might have developed over time, perhaps refined. After leaving school, Kenny admitted there had been limited inspiration working in a box factory.

'What did you do there?' I asked.

'Made boxes,' he said.

'How do you do that?'

'Christ on a bike, Rab. You have seen a fucking box, right?'

Kenny was only back in town that weekend for his cousin's going-away party.

'Where's he going?' I inquired.

'Bar-L,' Kenny said, perkily. 'Three years for assault and battery.'

This cousin, Johnny 'Genghis' McCann, had 'claimed' someone with a beer glass around back of The Wayfarer Lounge, smashing the sten against a wall, sticking the jaggy end in this person's cheek, corkscrewing and twisting it in.

> **It was Kenny I wanted to hear more about. I was intrigued to see how his poetic skills might have developed over time, perhaps refined**

'Smashed all his teeth out as well,' Kenny grinned wildly at me. 'Got him in a chokehold and kept smacking him on the gob with the glass till there was only his gums left. He'll be fine though.'

'He will?' I pawed at my mouth with my palms. 'After that?'

'Aye, he'll do just great. See my uncle Wullie is already up in Barlinnie for aggravated grievous bodily harm, so it'll be nice company for him.'

'Might have a touch of the psycho in him though, your cousin,' I speculated.

'Nah. He's dead nice so he is, good at Subbuteo also. A psycho would be the likes of that wanker Ronnie Bunting. Remember him? That headcase is in the Bar-L as well now. Wee pygmy went and shot his girlfriend.'

'Why?'

'She was annoying him.'

'I see.'

'The scuttlebutt is they had a donnybrook concerning this sex toy Ronnie bought. She suggested they should start off by him shoving it up his own arse. I didn't get the full story, just the gist. Only sex toy that vicious midget ever needed was a ladder.'

'I don't know anyone who's ever shot anyone,' I noted. 'Besides my father.'

'You must,' Kenny said, in disbelief. 'You live in America. They shoot each other over there to say hello. It's like Miami Vice so it is.'

'No, I seriously don't know anyone who's ever shot anyone.'

'I've shot people a lot,' Kenny observed, phlegmatically. 'So, you can tell folks you do know a shooter now.'

It was disconcerting, he said, having mortar shells flying about your head like that trifle Doc smacked you in the gob with that time

After his stint in the box factory, Kenny joined the army to see the world. Which explained the haircut. He'd been posted to Northern Ireland and taken potshots at IRA types sneaking over the border with trouble in mind, but it wasn't fun because the Tims skedaddled to the Republic and then fired back at you. 'It was disconcerting,' he said, 'having mortar shells flying about your head like that trifle Doc smacked you in the gob with that time.' He had not joined the army to be shot at. Presently, he was stationed in the Falkland Islands, where the army had a garrison to dissuade the Argentines from invading again. It was bloody awful. 'There was nothing to do,' he explained, 'on that remote ice-smote lump of sheep shit. There was no women, no drink, no TV, no entertainment, not even prospect of the Argies attacking. At least that would be interesting.'

'You know what we do for fun?' he asked.

'No,' I said, with some trepidation.

'You'll never guess.'

'Probably not. Does it involve bestiality?' I ventured, jokingly.

'Naw,' Kenny expostulated, looking very shocked. 'That was just that Corporal MacDonald that one time. The man was a bit on the lonely side I think. It was a downright shame his name wasn't McLeod instead though, eh?'

'How's that?'

'So as we could have shouted at him, you know, like how Mick Jagger does: "Hey McLeod, get offa mah ewe."'

'Ah,' I said. 'So, what is it you do do for fun then?'

'Doo-Doo,' Kenny said, cackling. Then it came, a bolt from the blue: a stunning utterance that remains for me still the absolute apotheosis of Kenny's poetic art. He announced, with a deep solemnity: 'We strap high explosives to the penguins.'

There was much that struck me about this line of original verse, besides the satisfying rhythm, and the element of surprise. It was that no one – in the history of spoken English – had ever before combined those words into that sequence. Kenny was still an original, a pure innovator, like a

Glaswegian Wallace Stevens. It was difficult for me also to contemplate any other combination of a mere seven words ('We strap high explosives to the penguins') that could encapsulate that much horror, that much humor, and that much revelation of deep, perhaps unfathomable, psychosis.

And he wasn't finished. I was for one night only in that manky pub given a rare glimpse of his creative genius. Me, a man from Porlock who didn't interrupt, but stimulated the muse on its road of excess to the Palace of Mayhem. I still maintain to this day that my presence evoked in the mature wordsmith that night one of the earliest known versions of freestyling in complete ten-beat units. This was to become Kenny's Kubla Khan, his Skylark or, maybe mostly, his Waste Land.

'Little fuckers would just waddle away.' Kenny looked off thoughtfully, over towards the mob of half-cut neds mule-kicking the jukebox and banging away on the pinball machine, perchance visualizing the last sojourn of his booby-trapped seafowl, searching for the perfect concluding line. The poet laureate of Glasgow took a last sup of lager, licked his lips, and found it: "Kaboom. We used to call them Pengrenades.' **H**

Short online creative writing courses

Book now for May!

- Study online at any time from the comfort of home
- Fully tutored, receive individual feedback on your work
- Small, friendly groups – 15 students max
- Beginner and intermediate levels available
- Co-designed with the University of East Anglia

'The materials were excellent and the tutor feedback was so helpful. I feel I have learned such a lot and my writing has definitely improved as a result.'

Lisa Tippings, Start Writing Creative Non-Fiction

nationalcentreforwriting.org.uk/creative-writing-online/

Boy

Next Door

by Jack Young

I.

He was, quite literally, the boy next door. He was everything my childhood self wanted to be: rebellious, strong and confident. His big house loomed at the top of the hill, above mine. My house was moon-blue and haunted, little-boy-me living with all of the adult things that were emerging inside. The boy next door was an escape, until the misty borders between the big things and the small began to blur.

Little hands scrambling on the tree between our houses, his fingers, rebellioustrongconfident, joined together, locked, thrusting me upwards. Up up up, towards the branches, towards the sky. The impossible sky, that impossible pure light, seen through the spaces between trees, branches twisting knotting receding. Our forest-thick little world. Shifting spaces between the big and the small.

I swing myself up, my skin becoming torn on the rough trunk as I scramble to get a hold. Safe on the ledge, I put my grazed fingers into my mouth and slowly lick my salt-sweat blood. It is a taste like no other: a taste of me. I look down at his face from this secret tree world and his smile is open wide, impressed. I feel meringue-puffed up then, swollen with pride. He quickly clambers behind – in two swift moves – with his dad's hammer tucked into the back of his mud-stained tracksuit bottoms.

We are bashing planks of wood into the old beech tree, the boy next door and me. It is a tree older than us, older than our parents, older than our parents' houses. Older than all of it; this knotted beech tree. It will live on long after we are gone. Yet for now we are building a house in the rafters, a house just for us, away from all the big things in the house moon-blue below. It feels so certain and powerful to be up here with the boy next door bashing rusty nails into ancient wood. Our fingers gentle-touching amongst the branches, plotting and scheming rebellion, away from the big people who order our lives below.

—

I was 10 going on 11, at primary school: the boy next door was 12 going on 13, at secondary. As a child such gaps seem huge and intangible, like a whole other life has been lived before you that you cannot even begin to understand. The vastness of that gap of one or two years when you are at the slippery borders of puberty, moving from a walk to primary school to getting the bus to secondary. Being split from your classmates for subjects and vomited out of the relatively collaborative feel of primary into a world of competition. Grades and sets; taught so early to turn against your peers. No more exploring. Time to grow up.

The boy next door was loud, obnoxious and full of disorder. We would run wildfire around the streets, knee-grazed, t-shirt stained and bodies worm-slippery moist, panting and alive. Knock-a-door-running-heart-in-mouth. The thrill of all that time! Time feeling stretched and supple, floating away from us like it never would again.

We grow up so fast, we forget who we were. We forget that floating time stretched like bubbles blown behind us...

Important blue things had been happening for as long as I could remember; deep-blue glances between my older sister and mum. Glances I could see but did not have a language to understand. When dad left us, all the blue things were a trail of destruction stretching behind him: a forest charred to its roots, held choking and dying after fire. We were part of that trail; my mum, my sister and me. We had to learn together how to find our way to a new forest, to somewhere safer than the one we found ourselves in after dad left. We had to learn to start again. I discovered the destructive power of men very early in my life.

We grow up so fast, we forget who we were. We forget that floating time stretched like bubbles blown behind us; so delicate, always already disappearing, yet so full of possibility while they are here in the now.

Our fingers gentle-touching amongst the branches,
love-pleached, bodies entwined, the spaces between
trees branches twisting knotting receding

We built our tree house; played hide and seek for
hours at the weekends; made storehouses of water
balloons on hot summer days; crawled through
the hedge to one another. Sometimes we met in
the hedge in the night, the potent smell of foxes
lingering in the air, heady and putrid, feeling so
unruly. In the day nesting like rabbits in a warren,
the sharp twigs of the hedge cocooning themselves
around our panting bodies, out of breath from all
the building and running and playing. Safe for a
little while. No matter how many borders the adults
put between us, we would be able to find our way
back to one another. We felt sure of that.

I was in awe as he told me of all the girls' breasts
he'd touched at his new school. I was desperate to
be as grown up as him. I was envious, though I
didn't know whether it was about the girls or him.
I had never kissed a girl at that point, but I had
kissed quite a few boys: Michael, Ryan, Duncan.
We batted them away as hilarious jokes, pathways
to somewhere else.

a taste like no other: a taste of me

The boy next door and me had sleepovers.
We could be anyone we wanted then, inventing
ourselves in wild and uncharted spaces.

twilight sheets cover gentle-breath bodies, sheets billow like clouds in our made-up sky, a sky beneath the big sky that if we think about too much makes us repeat our names over and over till we are sure that we are not really here at all. The impossible sky. The big of it all. A dream. Faces owl-huddled on the branches that are our bodies, whole spaces growing from whispered stories between. Murmured secrets in the twilight dark. The spaces between words, the looks, the breath, the touch, cocoon-pleached beneath twilight sheets. Murmurs of abandoned houses, unicorns lost in the woods, children trying to find their way back home. Torchlight turned upwards towards his grin, toothy and dazzling. Stars twinkle in forest-dark. A fox? A badger? A gloamglozer waiting for its prey?

I felt far away from the big blue things in my house in those moments, as we built our forest worlds. Away from the endless lies dad told as he fucked his way through the world, away from all his devastating power, his straight libido obliterating the needs of anyone else around him with his hunger.

But in our secret worlds, the boy next door and me, we were orange and purple and gold stitched upon the darkness – tapestries of endless stars – whole worlds of touch, erotic then but in a way that pre-exists the specifically sexual. The erotics of a child, existing as something with infinite possibilities. How it needn't be synonymous with the sexual, rather an ability to share intimacy and closeness; the comfort and power of a desired embrace as a child. I spent a lot of my childhood, I've since come to realise, craving more touch and affection. In many ways my sister was the opposite: she withdrew as her means to deal with all the blue things that had engulfed our little world, yet I craved this world of touch as a way to feel like I had something to hold onto, that the big people I loved might stay.

We go darker, deeper, much deeper than we have before. We are curious. Or *he* is curious. But am I?

Some of the times I felt most myself as a child was in the arms of my mum, or huddled up with the boy next door, hands gentle-touching amongst the branches. There is an erotic behind this kind of intimacy that need not always be pathologized; we grow far too quickly into detachment and withdrawal from physical connection. How much closer we might feel to our worlds and our bodies as teenagers if we perceived intimacy as a source of strength, if we were able to better articulate in the spaces between words.

One night, dream-like, in our forest sheets, the touching changes. We go darker, deeper, much deeper than we have before. We are curious. Or *he* is curious. But am I? It's hard to know now. Adult-time and all the years of burial have served to refract this memory beyond recognition.

In the dreamnotdream: who is the dreamer and who is the dreamed of? Who is touching and who is being touched?

*We are going to places we have never been before, to the
caves beneath our worlds, greenish with the ooze of time,
the dim light in the woods turning to mist, the owls have
flown away. All quiet. Forest-still. Breath meets breath in
the forest-thick. The spaces between trees, branches knotting,
twisting, wrapping themselves behind our bodies, concealing
the entrance to the cave we have passed through. Breath-
heavy in the mist, descending deeper, to places never touched
before. Places I have never thought about, not like this. There
is purpose to his touching, a fumbling towards something
that might lie beneath. We are lost beneath the woods in the
dreamnotdream and we don't know where we are going or
how we can get back. These touches do not have names yet,
these parts have lain hidden till now. A whole world opening
up. Unsure I'm ready. I am touching myself, and him, in
this dreamnotdream. My body does not speak to me, does not
feel much, but his says a lot, his seems so big and strong and
growing. To make him feel this much, this makes me feel a
power I have never felt before. A power over someone else.
Until now I have never felt power over anyone. I want to
impress him; I'm doing what I think he wants me to do.*

Rustling, fumbling, something spills in the mist, within the now sea-cave-slippery dark, something emptying out of myself

*We are not speaking, no, no. Not speaking. No words
anymore. The spaces between. All quiet. Breath meets breath
in the cave-dark. Touching, rustling, twilight sheets beneath
the forest. Stars distant memories, forest-floor carpeted above.
Rustling, fumbling, something spills in the mist, within
the now sea-cave-slippery dark, something emptying out of
myself. I am feeling so much but understanding so little.*

The next day we didn't speak of the cave, we never named what happened back then. I don't think we would've had the names even if we'd tried. How hard I find it to separate the 'I' from the 'We' as I write this, for the first time, as I try to give it language and form. How much did *I* want it? How much was it 'We' or 'He' or 'I'? For so long I have buried this. Our twilight secret. Rich and dark and intoxicating: the separation of self and other. He was so much bigger than me, in so many ways full of more of this. This desire, this want, these feelings we did not have the names for. I was too young to understand. But we did want it. He did want it. I did want it. Didn't I?

We were splitting apart, growing up too fast, as the 'I's' came stuttering forth, lost and bewildered. How confusing the sexual is as a child. The slippery, misty borders between the big things and the small. Another night:

We are two boys stealing into his parents' bedroom, those forbidden fortresses, taking condoms from their top drawers, momentary wanderers within their private worlds as I think to myself: now we know your grown-up world, now we have your night. We feel so powerful, but he is more powerful, and it feels like his power is growing beyond me, that his power is growing into something that he doesn't want to share anymore. It feels like the wildfire of him is engulfing us – our forest – and burning it to cinders.

Though I didn't realise it then, there would soon be only charred ground, with no space left for our love to grow.

*We are watching porn together in the computer room of his
house. I can't remember if it is men on the screen, or women,
or both: there is a blank screen in my memory where the
videos were. We are touching each other, exploring our bodies
as they stutter outwards, wildfire spreading everywhere,
flames licking relentlessly through the forest into the cave-
dark beneath. His mum walks in and we cover ourselves
quickly. She walks out, pretending not to see. He is red-faced
and angry: I am ashamed. I run home. He doesn't speak
to me for a week and I feel I am his dirty secret. All of this
unspoken, no names for what we are.*

For years these memories were obscured, like
the blank screen of the porn videos from my
recollection, until they started to unearth
themselves in recent years. These things I had
buried deep beneath my little world. It was way
before I understood those places, that more sexual
kind of erotic, where my body responded but I
couldn't understand. I was ten years old. How much
choice can you really have at that age over your
body and those cave-dark adult things?

Around the time of the incident in the computer
room, the sleepovers became less and less frequent.
He got a girlfriend and began to make new friends.
I eventually moved to comprehensive school and
began to make new friends of my own. I started
kissing girls. We forgot our secret twilight world
– the forest-thick gorgeousness reduced to the ash
of memory. His dad took down our abandoned
treehouse and no one would know, looking at the
old beech tree, that it had ever been there.

Those unspoken things with the boy next door bled into the abyss of the unknown. They have never found a form until now. Yet I felt I had experienced something way before my peers when I reached secondary school, discovered something too soon, and that I could never go back. When the nights shift from one kind of possibility – the child's forest imaginary – to the deeper, darker, more complex caverns of adult desire.

> **My desire to impress *him*... meant a pushing down of the queer desires that had begun to surface with the boy next door.**

How long have these desires been dormant? Left hidden in my pre-pubescent bedsheets. That dizzying, porous border between childhood and adolescence. In many ways he was my first love. Falling down together as we did into our cave and then emerging to find ourselves separate, moved on, grown up too fast. The boy next door and the worlds we built receding from view. The kisses of boys batted away as hilarious jokes, pathways to somewhere else.

II.

As I entered adolescence, I realised I had not escaped the charred forest left by my dad. My desire to impress *him* (no longer the boy next door) meant a pushing down of the queer desires that had begun to surface with the boy next door.

We are driving to McDonald's together; a secret treat mum would never allow, which makes it more exciting. I slouch down in the car seat and pull my cap over my head so I can only just see. I don't feel like talking but I also like that Dad thinks I am sleeping because it means I can watch him and take notes.

I notice his hands first, dry-stone strong on the wheel, before following his arms to his fleece-warm thick body. I glance up to his face next, where his teeth dazzle and his mouth is open wide, singing the words to the Manic Street Preachers song on the radio – if you tolerate this then your children will be next. *After a while I start singing along too, caught in the rush of him, though I have no idea what the lyrics mean. In these moments, he is curly, charming and beautiful. I want to bask in his power. So my mouth speaks words that I don't understand and my mouth copies his smile in the hope that I'll be able to capture a room like him one day.*

I was my dad's little secret, the only one who would visit him in his new life after he left us. I was desperate to know more of his secrets, to discover more of his power.

I am lying awake in the cramped spare room at his new place, brown patterned carpets swirl with swamp-green flowers, beer stained and mould crusted, the single bed creaking with broken springs.

I am his creaking little secret, sprung in single-bed coils, lying awake in the adult-dark. No one else will forgive him for the women and the leaving. I wait all week for our Friday Bond sessions, for our chats about 'Suave Moore'

and 'Banal Brosnan'. I don't know what 'suave' or 'banal'
mean, but I take note of them in my head so I can practice
them with my mates at school the following week, hoping
they'll be impressed.

It's just us for a while, until the faces of his new life join:
a steady stream of lovers that glide in and out of our burrow-
sunk world. When they begin to arrive, I hear strange noises
ghosting upwards from his bedroom at night as dull thuds
shudder up the walls.

I creep down then, peeping through the crack in his
bedroom door, slivers of the adult-dark that I'd already begun
to discover.

How I fell for his power. I adored him, was in awe
of him, wanted to matter enough that he might
continue to be a part of my life, that he might stick
around a little longer. I forgot the boy next door;
was taught by him, school, TV shows and films,
that desire ought to be directed towards things that
could be easily categorised and digested by society-
at-large. Like straightness. How much I did myself a
disservice in shutting off the queerer parts of myself,
and forgetting parts of who I was becoming, or
could be.

Dad's questions were all one-way traffic:

You got a girlfriend yet kiddo?

What's she like?

How about the Bond Girl this week?

They were closed questions, with only one way to look; through the cracks of his bedroom door. The door to elsewhere closed. Did he leave the door open on purpose? Was he worried my desires might not stay still?

Did he leave the door open on purpose? Was he worried my desires might not stay still?

He always seemed to have such confidence with his straightness, in terms of a life lived 'by his cock', to quote the phrase his best friend once used about him. Yet in spite of this apparent confidence, I remember how confused he always was by people who identified in varying non-normative ways to gender. He often said he could never understand, that he found it 'weird'. As I've reflected in later years, his reactions to non-normative gender identities show how threatened he found people who laid bare, in brave and beautiful terms, the fragility upon which the foundations of binary gender are built. Now I know this shows how vulnerable dominant power actually is, even when it seems insurmountable and becomes so much more aggressively asserted when under threat.

Yet how insidious and overarching straightness is. As an adult I've lost count of the times I've been forced to 'declare' a fixed sexuality by straight-identifying women seemingly interested in me, with the questions 'are you gay?' or 'are you straight?' I was aware it had often come from the women having been hurt by rejection in previous encounters, but it seems only patriarchy wins with such policing of sexuality, such obsession with some kind of 'disclosure'; as if sexuality is some fixed point or truth that we can reach. From my experience it's just so much messier and more incomplete than that. And every time I'm asked that question, that forced confessional, I feel it lacerating through my sense of who I feel I am. Of who I could be.

fingers gentle-touching amongst the branches, bodies entwined, the spaces between trees branches twisting knotting receding

III.

I am 13 years old, in the kitchen of the house I grew up in. Something is coming, something is lurking. I am looking at Dad's hands nervous and Mum's eyes strange, who has been telling me for the past week that this meeting will be important but has said nothing more.

Now he is telling me that he is going to die, that his bones dry-stone strong are breaking, that his insides are being gutted and fish-counter-splayed by a cancer that won't stop till its tentacles have wrapped themselves across every inch of his fleece-warm body. This kitchen holds many memories, many murmured conversations never had, haughty plates on shelves never used, though this perhaps is the bluest and his hands in his hair before it perished and my hands on his hands before they shrivelled, my legs sitting by his legs before they withered and the crying and the breaking and the crying and the hands.

He died five years later, when I was 18 years old. It has taken many years to reckon with that loss, both in terms of the destructive legacy of masculinity he mapped out while he was living, and the ghosts that have traced themselves onto my life since his death.

In losing my dad I lost the ability to hold him to account, at the very age my peers were breaking away in earnest from the influence of their parents and messily shaping a sense of who they wanted to be. I will always resent being denied an opportunity to begin to break from his influence as I left home and the city I grew up in, though of course I can never know what might have happened if he had lived.

Over time I have begun to move beyond the straitjacket enforced upon me by him and his world. My teenage years involved plenty of hidden queer hook-ups and the follow-up rejection and shame. Yet what has changed is my desires now move more freely beyond his legacy, as I have learned to explore the boundlessness of love stripped from narrow categories of gender and sexuality. I wish to think beyond such narrow categories which, in my own experience, attempt to taxonomize the thing that resists taxonomy the most: the messy, incomplete, ever-shifting nature of desire.

I have never felt more beauty or power than when I explore the queer parts of myself; the curls of my eyelashes licked with mascara, sashaying, all snake-hipped and glamorous, in gold sequins beneath flickering lights at a club. My body splitting across the room in these reflections. I am mirror-ball mesmerising then, with the words of New

Order *every time I see you falling* pulsating through my whole being.

> **I am both in my body
> and out of my body...
> And it tastes and feels like freedom.**

In those moments I am *falling falling* back in the forest-dark. It is salt-blood-sweat-earth and endless stars, all at once. I am both in my body and out of my body. Both more myself than ever and something entirely strange. And it tastes and feels like freedom. In those moments I am walking away from the charred forest left by my dad. I'm entering a different wood, with the caves beneath me opening up, somewhere in the distance the boy next door is murmuring my name, and I am loving with nuance, across and beyond gender. **H**

Like what you've read?

Sign up for a subscription and get our next batch of stand-out writing delivered direct to your door, desktop or tablet.

Annual print & digital subscription £40
Four issues, p&p free

Annual digital subscription £20
Four issues, saving £4 off list price

Subscribers also enjoy the benefit of being able to submit their writing to Hinterland free of charge.

Visit our website to subscribe:

www.hinterlandnonfiction.com/subscribe